Challenge Your Mind
Math Games
Throughout the Year

by
Cindy Karwowski

Cover Design by
Vickie Lane

Inside Art by
Barb Lorseyedi

Publishers
Instructional Fair • TS Denison
Grand Rapids, Michigan 49544

Permission to Reproduce

Credits

Author: Cindy Karwowski
Cover Design: Vickie Lane
Inside Illustrations: Barb Lorseyedi
Project Director/Editor: Linda Kimble
Editors: Lisa Hancock, Sharon Kirkwood
Typesetting/layout: Pat Geasler

About the Author

Cindy Karwowski is a creative author and teacher. She has twice been a finalist for Michigan Teacher of the Year. After completing a Bachelor's degree at Carthage College in Kenosha, WI, Cindy began teaching elementary school. She continued her schooling by completing a Master's degree at Michigan State University.

Standard Book Number: 1-56822-782-5
Challenge Your Mind
Copyright © 1998 by Instructional Fair • TS Denison
2400 Turner Avenue NW
Grand Rapids, Michigan 49544

All Rights Reserved • Printed in the USA

Table of Contents

It All Begins in January

name _____

New Year's Day

Use the Word Bank to complete this calendar page.

January						
Sun.	**Mon.**	**Tues.**	**Wed.**	**Thurs.**	**Fri.**	**Sat.**
				one	two	three
_____ A	five	_____ B	_____ C	eight	nine	_____ D
_____ E	_____ I	thirteen	_____ M	_____ N	sixteen	seventeen
eighteen	_____ R	twenty	twenty- _____ S	twenty- _____ T	twenty-three	twenty-four
twenty- _____ U	twenty-six	twenty-seven	twenty- _____ Y	twenty-nine	thirty	thirty-one

Word Bank

eight
eleven
fifteen
five
four
nineteen
fourteen
one
seven
six
ten
twelve
two

Now use the number words on the calendar to write the letters that answer the riddle.

Why does a calendar feel sad on New Year's Eve?

___ ___ ___ ___ ___ ___ ___   ___ ___ ___
 6   11   7   4   25   21   11   12   22   21

___ ___ ___ ___   ___ ___ ___
10   4   28   21   4   19   11

___ ___ ___ ___ ___ ___ ___ ___ !
15   25   14   6   11   19   11   10

4

IF8721 *Challenge Your Mind*

Countdown

name _____

It's getting close to midnight!

Color the clock **yellow** if there are 50–55 minutes before midnight.

Color the clock **blue** if there are 35–45 minutes before midnight.

Color the clock **green** if there are 20–30 minutes before midnight.

Color the clock **red** if there are 5–15 minutes before midnight.

Color the clock **purple** if it is **midnight**.

© Instructional Fair • TS Denison

IF8721 *Challenge Your Mind*

Peace March

Name _____

Martin Luther King, Jr., was born on January 15, 1929. In 1963, Dr. King led over 250,000 people to the Lincoln Memorial and spoke of living together in peace.

Mark the marcher's path by coloring all footsteps that equal 15.

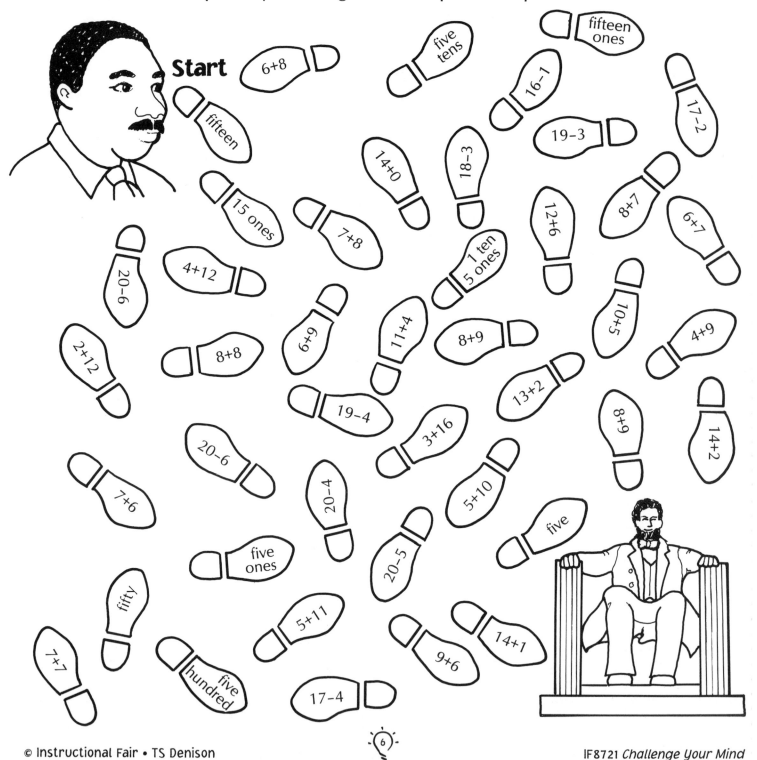

Start

6+8
fifteen
five tens
fifteen ones
16−1
19−3
17−2
15 ones
14+0
18−3
12+6
8+7
6+7
20−6
4+12
7+8
1 ten 5 ones
2+12
8+8
6+9
11+4
8+9
10+5
4+9
19−4
13+2
8+9
14+2
20−6
3+16
20−4
5+10
7+6
five ones
20−5
five
fifty
5+11
14+1
7+7
five hundred
9+6
17−4

6

We Go Together

name _____

Can you find the missing fact from each family?

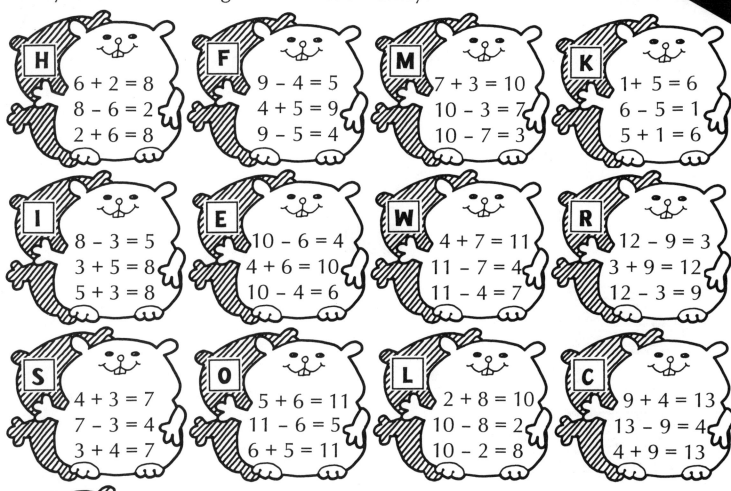

H
6 + 2 = 8
8 – 6 = 2
2 + 6 = 8

F
9 – 4 = 5
4 + 5 = 9
9 – 5 = 4

M
7 + 3 = 10
10 – 3 = 7
10 – 7 = 3

K
1+ 5 = 6
6 – 5 = 1
5 + 1 = 6

I
8 – 3 = 5
3 + 5 = 8
5 + 3 = 8

E
10 – 6 = 4
4 + 6 = 10
10 – 4 = 6

W
4 + 7 = 11
11 – 7 = 4
11 – 4 = 7

R
12 – 9 = 3
3 + 9 = 12
12 – 3 = 9

S
4 + 3 = 7
7 – 3 = 4
3 + 4 = 7

O
5 + 6 = 11
11 – 6 = 5
6 + 5 = 11

L
2 + 8 = 10
10 – 8 = 2
10 – 2 = 8

C
9 + 4 = 13
13 – 9 = 4
4 + 9 = 13

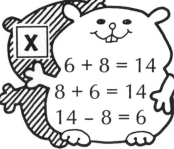

X
6 + 8 = 14
8 + 6 = 14
14 – 8 = 6

To solve the riddle write the letter on the groundhog's shadow that matches the missing fact.

What do you get when you cross a groundhog with your principal?

7–4 = 3	8–5= 3	14–6= 8		3+7= 10	11–5= 6	9+3= 12	6+4= 10

7+4 = 11	6+4= 10	6+4= 10	6–1= 5	7–4 = 3		11–5= 6	5+4= 9

7–4= 3	13–4= 9	8–2= 6	11–5= 6	11–5= 6	8+2= 10

IF8721 *Challenge Your Mind*

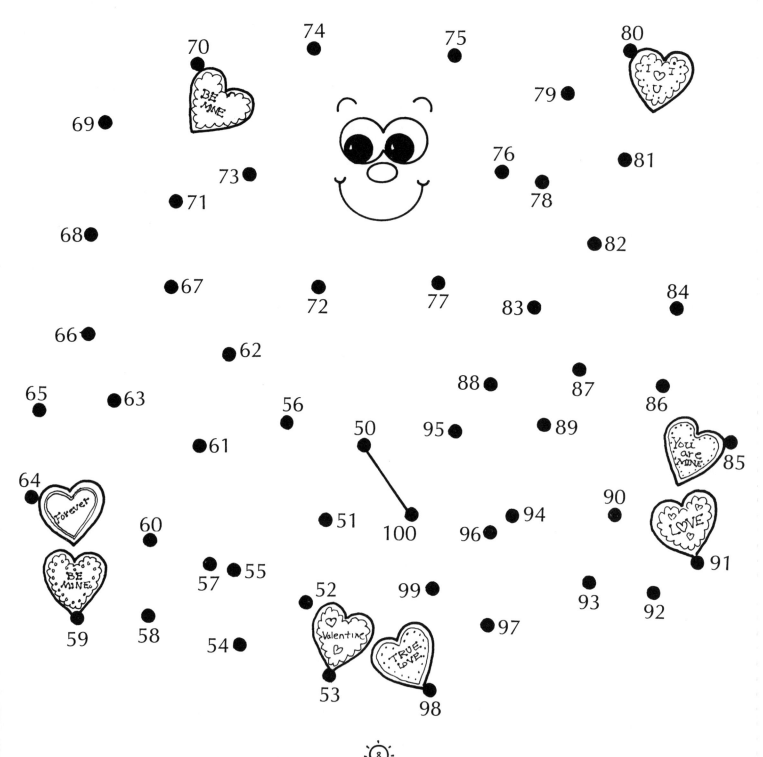

Armloads of Valentines

name _____

Valentine's Day

Connect the dots by counting from 50 to 100. Who has lots of valentines to deliver?

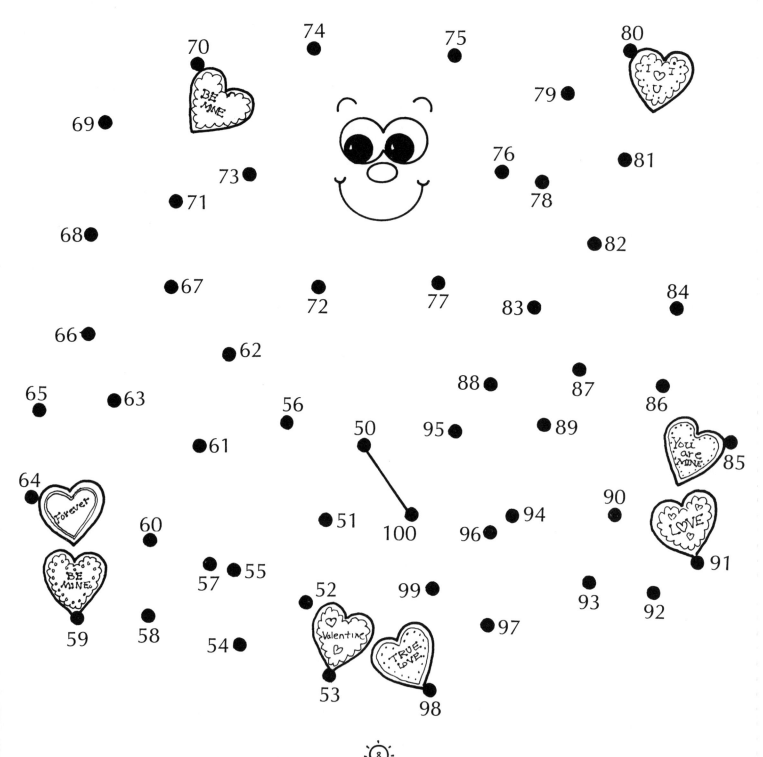

Heart to Heart

Name _____

Recopy each group of hearts in order from smallest to largest to answer each riddle. Write both the numbers and the words.

What happened to the Valentine sweethearts who wanted to kiss in the fog?

mist 501
They 349
tried 361
they 482
but 411

How do you kiss a hockey player?

You 158
pucker 217
need 179
up 270
to 190

What did the postage stamp say to the envelope on Valentine's Day?

I 87
stuck 101
on 110
you 115
am 96

What did the snake say to his special sweetie?

me 37
a 41
little 54
58 hiss
Give 23

9

Hidden Surprise

name _____

To discover the filling in each chocolate candy, solve each problem and then color each piece correctly.

46	=	cherry (red)		54	=	lime (green)
37	=	lemon (yellow)		68	=	blueberry (blue)
75	=	orange (orange)		83	=	solid chocolate (brown)

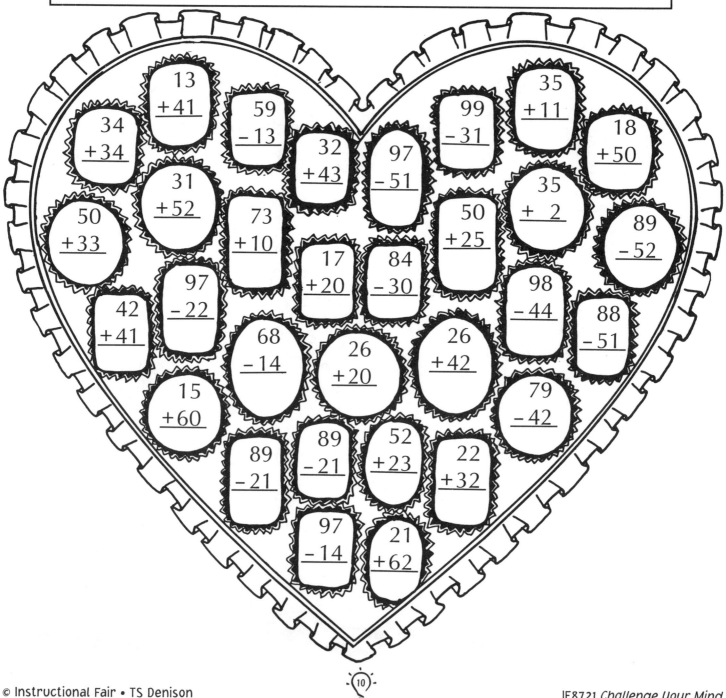

© Instructional Fair • TS Denison

IF8721 *Challenge Your Mind*

Name _____

Valentine's Day

Use a **red** crayon to color all of the spaces with **odd numbers**. Then begin at the ♥ and write the letters that are **not** colored in the hearts below. Be sure to follow the letters in order.

How do you know when two boa constrictors are in love?

11

Love Pranks

Name _____

Cupid has been busy shooting his love arrows. Add the numbers in the hearts. Then, draw lines to the hearts that match to discover who Cupid's arrows hit.

9 5 7 2

2 4 12

1 8 7 3

2 7 4 6

9 8 10 7

7 6 10

9 9 7 4 5

5 7 8 5

4 6 5 3

9 3 5 8

IF8721 *Challenge Your Mind*

Royal Tarts

name _____

Follow each path from the Queen of Hearts to her royal cousins. Discover how many tarts she made for each of them for Valentine's Day. Write that number on their crowns.

Mending Broken Hearts

name _____

Mend the broken hearts by coloring the matching halves the same color. You will need **six** different colors.

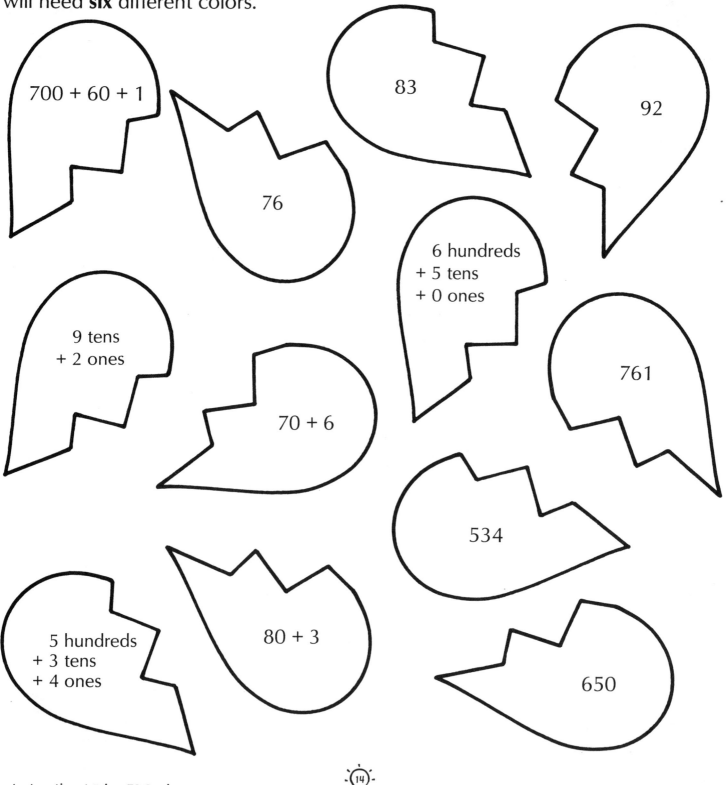

700 + 60 + 1

83

92

76

9 tens
+ 2 ones

6 hundreds
+ 5 tens
+ 0 ones

761

70 + 6

534

5 hundreds
+ 3 tens
+ 4 ones

80 + 3

650

© Instructional Fair • TS Denison

IF8721 *Challenge Your Mind*

Presidential Humor

name _____

Presidents Day

Solve the subtraction problems. Match the letters to the answers beneath each line to find out which president had the most children.

A 18 − 9	B 6 − 6	C 10 − 2	E 8 − 7
F 11 − 9	G 15 − 9	H 12 − 9	I 10 − 5
N 14 − 7	O 9 − 5	R 20 − 10	S 16 − 3
T 14 − 2	U 15 − 0	W 18 − 7	Y 16 − 2

____ ____ ____ ____ ____ ____ ____ ____ ____ ____ ,
11   9   13   3   5   7   6   12   4   7

____ ____ ____ ____ ____ ____ ____   ____ ____
0   1   8   9   15   13   1   3   1

____ ____ ____ ____ ____ ____ ____ ____ ____ ____ ____ ____
11   9   13   12   3   1   2   9   12   3   1   10

____ ____ ____ ____ ____ ____ ____ ____ ____ ____ ____ ____
4   2   4   15   10   8   4   15   7   12   10   14

© Instructional Fair • TS Denison

15

IF8721 *Challenge Your Mind*

Color Me Lucky

Name _____

Solve each problem and write the answer next to it.

If the number is < 20, color it **green**.

If the number is = 20, color it **orange**.

If the number is > 20, color it **tan**.

© Instructional Fair • TS Denison

IF8721 *Challenge Your Mind*

Lucky Numbers

name _____

This leprechaun's lucky number is 9.

Color the shamrock **green** if the 9 is in the **hundreds place**.

Color the shamrock **yellow** if the 9 is in the **tens place**.

Color the shamrock **orange** if the 9 is in the **ones place**.

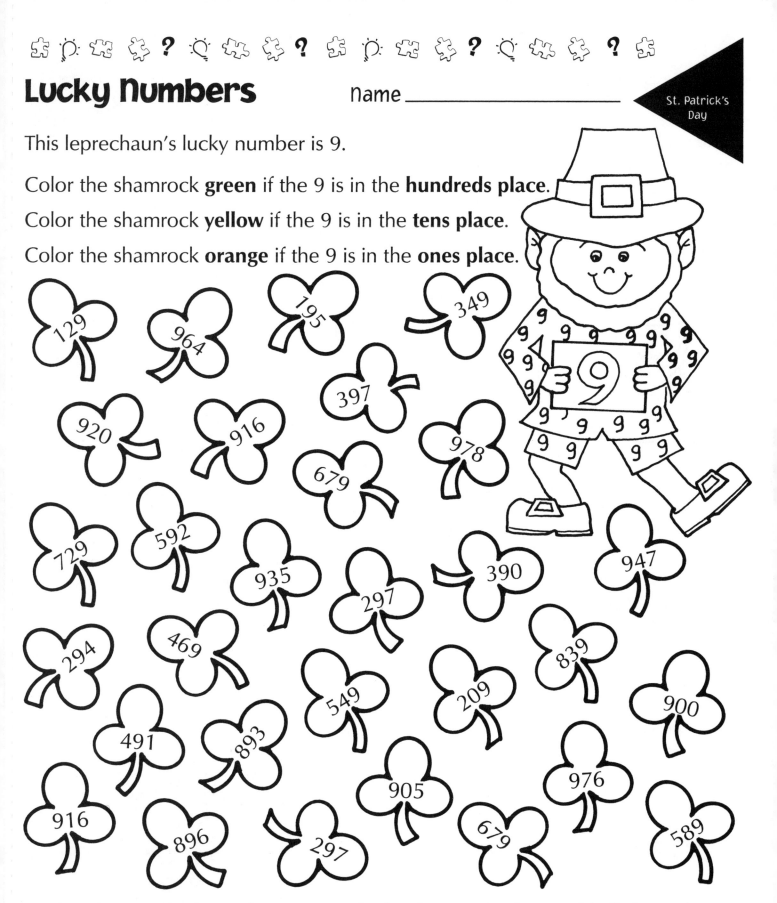

Find and circle the leprechaun's very lucky shamrock. If you add all three digits of this shamrock together, you will get nine.

Golden Names

name _____

St. Patrick's Day

Write and solve the number problems by matching the letters in each name with the correct number.

If a leprechaun's name indicates his worth in gold, how many coins of gold is each leprechaun worth? Then color the leprechaun whose name is worth the most.

A	I	E	L	N	O	D	S	T	Y	U	R
1	2	3	4	5	6	7	8	9	10	11	12

LADDY

LOUIE

4 + 1 + 7 + 7 + 10 = 29 _____

LENNIE

_____

LESLIE

_____

LENNON

_____

LESTER

_____

IF8721 *Challenge Your Mind*

Pure Gold

name _____

Help the leprechaun sort his genuine gold coins from the fake ones. Color the coin **golden** (yellow) if the number on it is **even**. Color the coin **brown** if the number is **odd**.

Pots O' Gold

name _____

St. Patrick's Day

How many coins does each leprechaun have in his pot? Read the clues and write the number on the pot.

The number of my coins is an even number. It is greater than 50 and less than 62. The sum of its two digits is 13.

My coins are a factor of 5. I have less than 60 coins. The sum of its two digits is 10.

I'm glad I have 3 more coins than the second highest leprechaun.

I have saved an odd number of coins. It is half of 100 plus 17.

I've collected more than 65 coins but less than 75. The sum of its two digits is 11. The first digit is larger than the second.

IF8721 *Challenge Your Mind*

Golden Feet

Name _____

Begin at **50** and count by **10s**. Write the corresponding letters in that order in the shamrocks to answer this question:

What would happen if a leprechaun jogged into a field of four-leaf clovers?

E	H
60	50

L	D	O	U	W
100	110	80	90	70

A	H	E	V
130	120	150	140

A
160

U	N	R
180	190	170

F	O
210	200

O	D	G	O
230	250	220	240

C	U	K	L
280	270	290	260

IF8721 *Challenge Your Mind*

Rainbow of Colors

Name _____

Help the leprechaun climb over the rainbow to reach his pot of gold.
Solve each addition problem. Then look at the first three boxes in a row.
Which one equals 2? Color it any color. Climb to the next three boxes. Which
one equals 4? Color it another color. Continue counting by 2s until you reach
the pot of gold. Try to use a different color for each row.

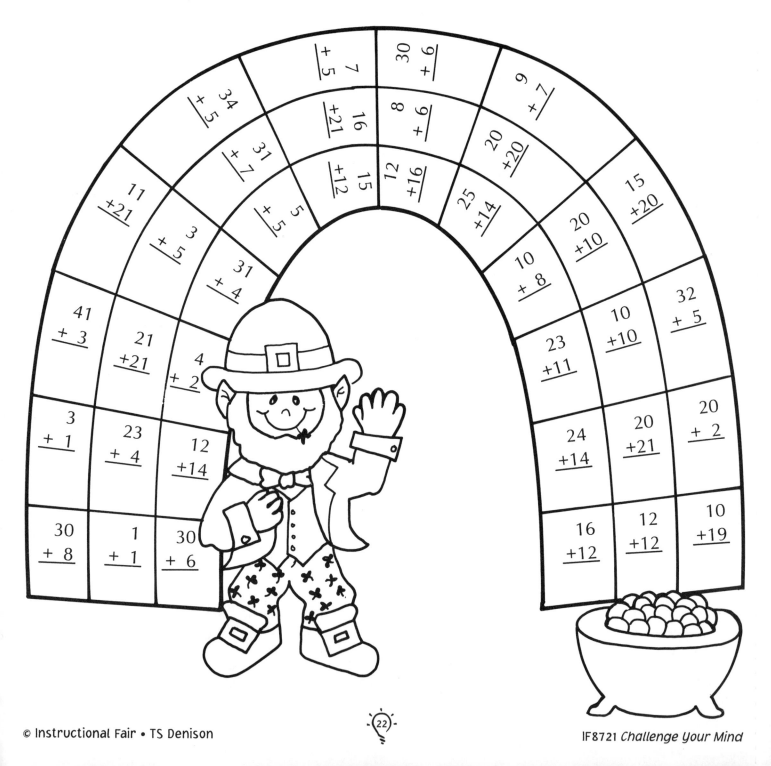

© Instructional Fair • TS Denison

IF8721 *Challenge Your Mind*

Count the Coins

name _____

St. Patrick's Day

Each whole pot of gold contains $1.00. Count the money in each half and write the amount on the pot. Then draw a line to connect the two halves that equal $1.00.

Easter Mix-Up

Name _____

Find out what you get . . .
when you cross a baby Easter chick and a baby Easter bunny.

Cut out the squares at the bottom of this page and paste them onto the boxes with the same number. (Bold lines show the top of the square.)

1	**2**	**3**	**4**	**5**
6	**7**	**8**	**9**	**10**
11	**12**	**13**	**14**	**15**

seven	fourteen	ten	eight	three
thirteen	five	twelve	one	fifteen
two	eleven	four	nine	six

It's a Draw!

name _____

A **line of symmetry** shows that one half will be exactly the same as the other half.

Finish drawing these pictures by making both halves the same. Use the grid lines as a guide.

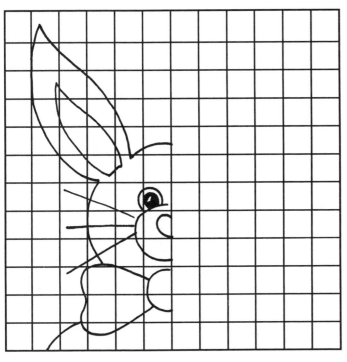

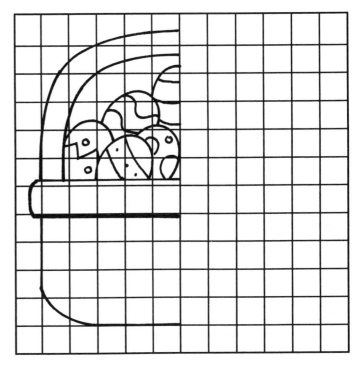

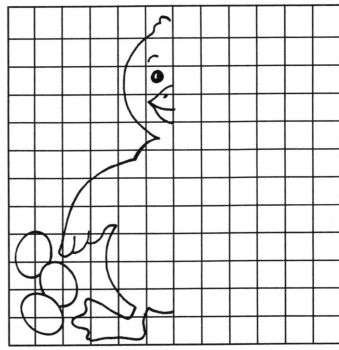

Mystery Eggs

Name _____

Easter

Write the missing numbers in each mystery egg. Multiply the numbers both down (↓) and across (→) and get the third number as a product.

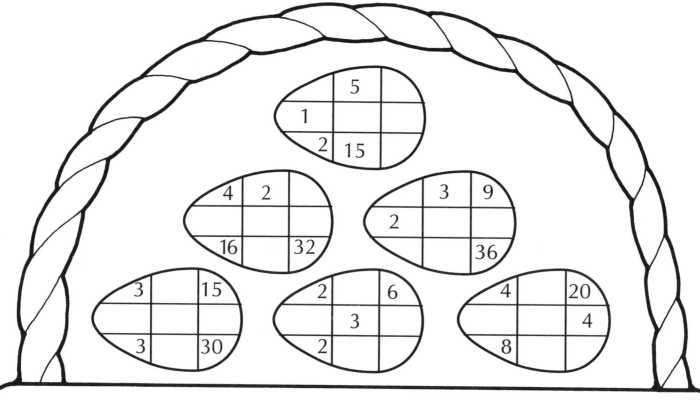

Count by 3s and write the letters in the correct order.

What is inside each mystery egg?

N	T	O	I	G	H	N
18	9	6	15	21	12	3

H	T	E
27	24	30

_____ _____ _____ _____ _____ _____ _____   _____ _____ _____ .

L	O	Y	K
39	36	33	42

S	I
48	45

N	O
54	51

U	Y	O
63	57	60

_____ _____ _____ _____   _____ _____   _____ _____   _____ _____ _____ !

Duck...Duck...Chick! name _____

Easter

Draw a line from a duck in the first column to a duck in the second column to a chick in the third column to form a division sentence. Use a different color for each problem.

16 ÷

9 ÷

30 ÷

21 ÷

72 ÷

5 =

4 =

9 =

7 =

8 =

3

1

9

6

4

IF8721 *Challenge Your Mind*

"Eggstra" Big Eggs

name _____

Put the eggs in order from largest to smallest. Write the numbers on the eggs below each basket.

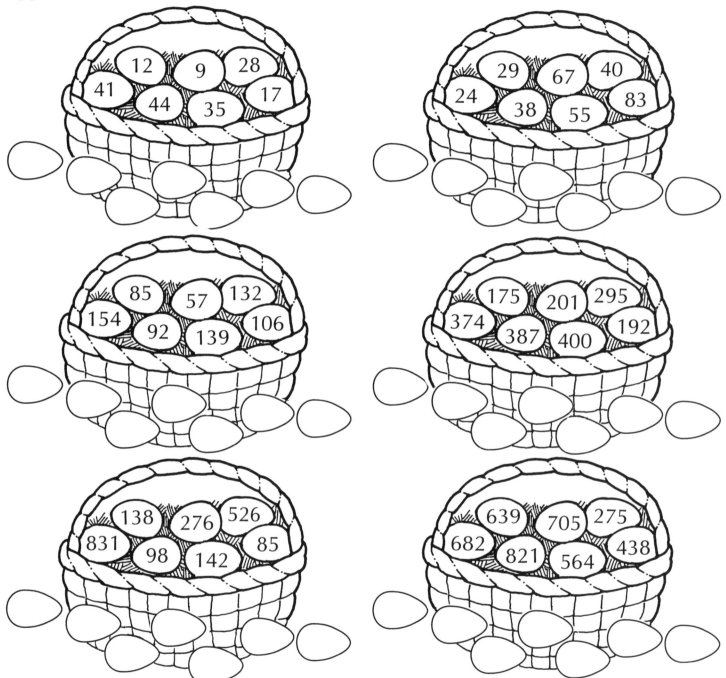

Basket 1: 12, 9, 28, 41, 44, 35, 17

Basket 2: 29, 67, 40, 24, 38, 55, 83

Basket 3: 85, 57, 132, 154, 92, 139, 106

Basket 4: 175, 201, 295, 374, 387, 400, 192

Basket 5: 138, 276, 526, 831, 98, 142, 85

Basket 6: 639, 705, 275, 682, 821, 564, 438

Now put the **largest** egg from each basket in order from largest to smallest.

Dozen It Make Sense?

Name _____

Read each clue. Then color eggs in each carton as directed.

3 blue eggs.   2 yellow eggs.
All of the rest are green and pink.
There is 1 more pink egg than green.

2 purple eggs.
There are twice as many green eggs as purple.
There are 3 times as many yellow eggs as purple.

3 pink eggs.
There is 1 more yellow egg than pink. There is one more orange egg than yellow.

There are the same number of blue and green eggs.
2 purple eggs.

4 times as many yellow eggs as green, 4 blue eggs.
1 less purple egg than blue.

3 red eggs.
There are twice as many blue eggs as red.
There are half as many yellow eggs as blue.

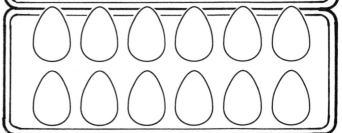

IF8721 *Challenge Your Mind*

Joking Around

name _____

What do you call ducks in a crate? A box of quackers!

Begin at **50** and count by 5s. Write the letters on the eggs in that order, and you will answer the question:

What happened when the Easter Bunny told a bunch of silly jokes?

l	a	l
60	50	55

f	o
70	65

e	t	h
85	75	80

g	s	e	g
95	105	90	100

e	c	k	r	a	c	d
135	125	130	115	120	110	140

p	u
150	145

Now connect the dots in the same order.

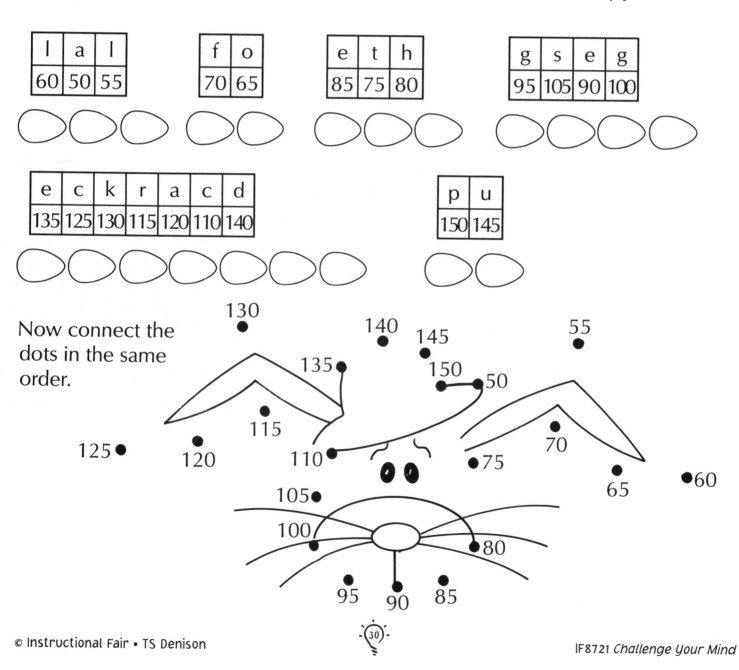

© Instructional Fair • TS Denison

IF8721 *Challenge Your Mind*

Quadruplets

name _____

Easter

Solve each problem. Write the answer on the jellybean. Find each set of **four** jellybeans whose answers are equal and color them the same color. You will need **six** different colors.

© Instructional Fair • TS Denison

IF8721 *Challenge Your Mind*

Cracked Eggs

name _____

Easter

Match the two pieces of eggs that have equal sums by coloring each half the same color. You will need eight different colors.

Coloring Easter Eggs Name _____

Solve each multiplication fact. Then color the picture by matching the answers with the colors.

orange

9
x 3

5   6
x 2   x 4

yellow

6
x 6

5   4
x 5   x 3

red

8
x 8

9   7
x 9   x 3

green

2
x 8

4   10
x 8   x10

brown

8
x 7

9   7
x 0   x 4

purple

5
x 9

3   6
x 3   x 8

white

2
x 7

6   5
x 3   x 8

blue

4
x 5

8   6
x 9   x 7

IF8721 *Challenge Your Mind*

Jellybean Countdown

Name _____

Read the clues and write the number of jellybeans on each line. Color the basket of jellybeans when you have answered the number riddles.

Red

I am an odd number between 10 and 20.

The sum of my 2 digits is 6.

I am _____ .

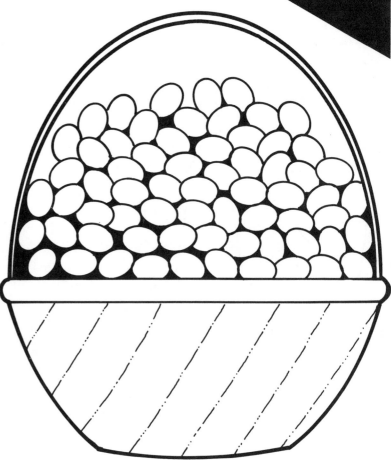

Yellow

I am an even number less than 10 and greater than 7.

I am _____ .

Green

I am an odd number less than 20 but greater than 15.

The sum of my 2 digits is 8.

I am _____ .

Blue

I am an even number less than 18.

I am divisible by both 4 and 6.

I am _____ .

Black

I am divisible by both 7 and 2.

I am less than 20.

I am _____ .

-34-

IF8721 *Challenge Your Mind*

Special Dinner

name _____

April Fool's Day

"Billy, why is my spaghetti moving?" asked little sister Tonya.

"I don't know what you mean," snickered Billy.

Use your noodle. Add all **six** numbers on each worm and write your answer on its head. (**Hint:** All of the numbers on each worm are different.)

IF8721 *Challenge Your Mind*

No Business Like
Shoe Business

Name _____

April Fool's
Day

Oh, no! A prankster took everyone's tennis shoes and threw them into a big pile.
Now they need to be arranged in pairs. Each pair of shoes contains a pair
of **consecutive numbers** (like 256, 257 or 921, 922). Write the numbers for each
pair on the lines below.

_____ , _____   _____ , _____   _____ , _____

_____ , _____   _____ , _____   _____ , _____

_____ , _____   _____ , _____   _____ , _____

_____ , _____

IF8721 *Challenge Your Mind*

Real Cut-Ups

name _____

This is confusing! Someone cut flash cards in half. Put them back together by writing each addition or subtraction fact on the blank cards below.

© Instructional Fair • TS Denison   IF8721 *Challenge Your Mind*

R-R-R-R-Ring!

name _____

April Fool's
Day

"Hello. Is your refrigerator running?"

"Yes."

"Then you'd better hurry and catch it or you won't have dinner tonight!"

Stop the refrigerator by finding the mistake it made while running away. Color that space **red**.

© Instructional Fair • TS Denison

·38·

IF8721 *Challenge Your Mind*

name _____

Begin at **68** and count backwards by 2s. Write the letters in that order on the bugs, and you will answer the question:

What has two heads, twenty-four legs, and sharp, pointy teeth?

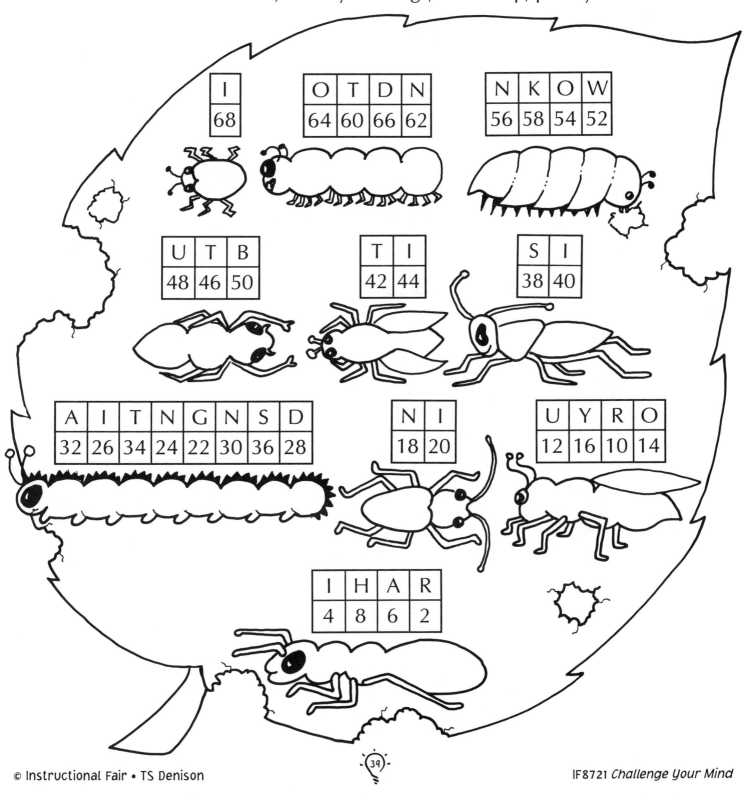

I
68

O	T	D	N
64	60	66	62

N	K	O	W
56	58	54	52

U	T	B
48	46	50

T	I
42	44

S	I
38	40

A	I	T	N	G	N	S	D
32	26	34	24	22	30	36	28

N	I
18	20

U	Y	R	O
12	16	10	14

I	H	A	R
4	8	6	2

IF8721 *Challenge Your Mind*

Quit Buggin' Me!

name _____

Placing candy bugs in clever places is one fun way to trick your friends. Color each matching half of a bug the same color. You will need **six** different colors.

- seventy
- 3 tens + 6 ones
- 7 tens
- 8 tens + 3 ones
- 9 tens + 6 ones
- seventeen
- thirty-six
- ninety-six
- 1 ten + 7 ones
- forty-eight
- eighty-three
- 4 tens + 8 ones

IF8721 *Challenge Your Mind*

Changing Places

name _____

Are you easily fooled?

Look **carefully** at the numbers. Write **ten** 3-digit number combinations inside the light bulbs using these numbers. One number may need to be flipped.

861

The Ol' Spider Joke

name _____

"Oh, no! There's a giant, furry, ugly spider crawling up
your back, and it's making a huge web!"

"Yeah, right!"

Discover the pattern in the spider web and fill in the missing numbers.
No connecting numbers are ever the same.

Love Our Planet

Name _____

Use a **blue** crayon to color all of the spaces with **odd numbers**. Then begin at the ★. Write the letters that are **not** colored in the spaces below in the same clockwise order.

___ ___ ___ ___   ___ ___ ___   ___ ___ ___ ___

___ ___ ___   ___ ___ ___   ___ ___

___ ___ ___ ___ ___ ___ ___ ___ ___ !

IF8721 *Challenge Your Mind*

Save Our Water!

name _____

Earth Day

Circle the word in each raindrop that comes **first** when counting. Then write its letter on the matching line below.

o second fourth

W fifth third

y first fourth

n fifteenth fourteenth

P seventh ninth

B twelfth eighth

T thirteenth fourteenth

K tenth eleventh

H ninth thirteenth

G ninth fourth

A fourteenth eleventh

I fifth eighth

S tenth sixth

E twelfth thirteenth

How do some children want to conserve water?

| 13th | 9th | 12th | 1st | | 3rd | 11th | 14th | 13th | | 13th | 2nd |

| 6th | 13th | 2nd | 7th | | 13th | 11th | 10th | 5th | 14th | 4th |

| 8th | 11th | 13th | 9th | 6th | **!** |

Happy Birthday

name _____

Arbor Day

Solve the problems. Then add the five sums in the tree rings to find the age of each tree. Write this number on the line.

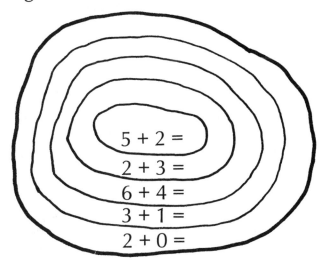

5 + 2 =
2 + 3 =
6 + 4 =
3 + 1 =
2 + 0 =

Age: _____ years

3 + 4 =
1 + 4 =
4 + 5 =
3 + 3 =
1 + 3 =

Age: _____ years

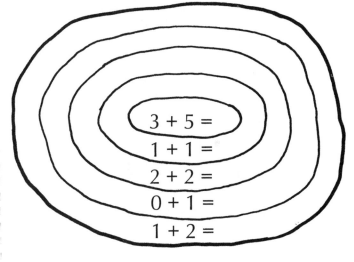

3 + 5 =
1 + 1 =
2 + 2 =
0 + 1 =
1 + 2 =

Age: _____ years

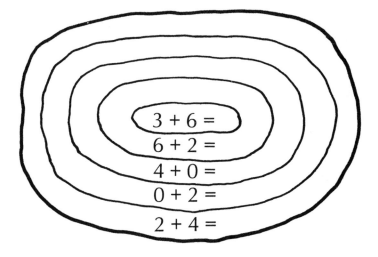

3 + 6 =
6 + 2 =
4 + 0 =
0 + 2 =
2 + 4 =

Age: _____ years

Color the ring **black** if the sum in a ring is **1 or 2**.

Color the ring **brown** if the sum in a ring is **3 or 4**.

Color the ring **green** if the sum in a ring is **5 or 6**.

Color the ring **yellow** if the sum in a ring is **7 or 8**.

Color the ring **orange** if the sum in a ring is **9 or 10**.

IF8721 *Challenge Your Mind*

Tree-mendous Riddles

name _____

Use a calculator to answer the riddles. Remember to press the equal sign after each direction and flip the calculator at the end to read the answer.

Question: What does Smokey the Bear always bring when he visits the forest?

Enter: the number of legs on a bear

×	900
−	ninety-six
+	.514
=	↻

Answer: _____

Question: Who visited the apple tree on a beautiful spring day?

Enter: the number of pennies in five dollars

×	ten
+	340
−	1.8782
=	↻

Answer: _____

Question: What did the maple tree do when it wanted syrup on its pancakes?

Enter: the number of one dozen trees

X	300
+	four hundred fifty
−	850
=	↻

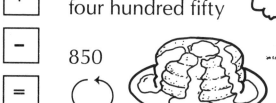

Answer: _____

Question: What do you call a tree that has stopped growing?

Enter: number before seventy

X	ten
+	seven
−	90
=	↻

Answer: _____

Home Sweet Home

name _____

Follow the path and solve the problems to discover the number of trees in this forest.

Start   7   ×   7   +   7

+   6   ×   8   ÷

8   ÷   5   +   5   ×

Answer   =   10   +   6

IF8721 *Challenge Your Mind*

Mother's Day Bouquet

name _____

Mother's Day

Write each missing number.

Color the space **yellow** if the number is **1–5**.

Color the space **purple** if the number is **6–10**.

Color the space **orange** if the number is **11–15**.

Color the space **red** if the number is **16–20**.

Color the space **green** if the number is **21–25**.

© Instructional Fair • TS Denison

IF8721 *Challenge Your Mind*

Mother Dear

name _____

Use a calculator to answer the questions. Remember to press the equal sign after each direction and flip the calculator at the end to read the answer.

Question: Who is one of the most famous mothers in history?

Enter: number of tentacles on an octopus

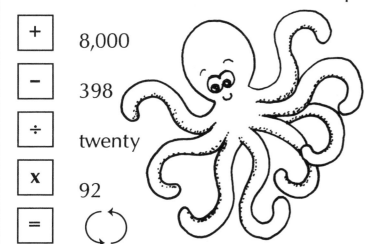

+	8,000
-	398
÷	twenty
x	92
=	↻

Answer: _____

Question: What mother doesn't lecture her child for "piggy" table manners?

Enter: number of pennies in 3 quarters

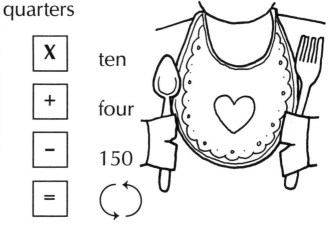

X	ten
+	four
-	150
=	↻

Answer: _____

Question: What did her children say as she read her favorite nursery rhymes?

Enter: the number of inches in one foot

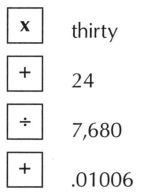

x	thirty
+	24
÷	7,680
+	.01006
=	↻

Answer: _____

Question: What did this famous mother call her first child?

Enter: number of years in a century

x	six
÷	two
-	134.0955
x	four
=	↻

Answer: _____

Honor Veterans

name _____

Solve these addition problems. Then match the letters on each star to the answers on the lines below.

I 2 + 6 + 3 = ____

P 2 + 1 + 2 = ____

M 7 + 2 + 4 = ____

C 4 + 6 + 6 = ____

Y 5 + 6 + 1 = ____

S 5 + 4 + 6 = ____

A 2 + 3 + 1 = ____

O 2 + 3 + 4 = ____

N 1 + 0 + 2 = ____

R 9 + 6 + 4 = ____

B 3 + 1 + 0 = ____

D 8 + 6 + 4 = ____

H 3 + 3 + 4 = ____

T 1 + 0 + 1 = ____

V 7 + 6 + 4 = ____

L 5 + 6 + 3 = ____

E 2 + 1 + 4 = ____

W 3 + 3 + 2 = ____

Why do Americans celebrate Memorial Day?

___ ___
2   9

___ ___ ___ ___ ___ ___ ___ ___ ___
16   7   14   7   4   19   6   2   7

___ ___ ___ ___ ___   ___ ___ ___
5   7   6   16   7   6   3   18

___ ___ ___ ___ ___   ___ ___ ___ ___ ___
10   9   3   9   19   2   10   9   15   7

___ ___ ___   ___ ___ ___ ___   ___ ___
8   10   9   18   11   7   18   11   3

___ ___ ___ ___ .
8   6   19   15

50

IF8721 *Challenge Your Mind*

Boom!

name _____

Think big! Solve each subtraction problem. Then check them with a calculator.

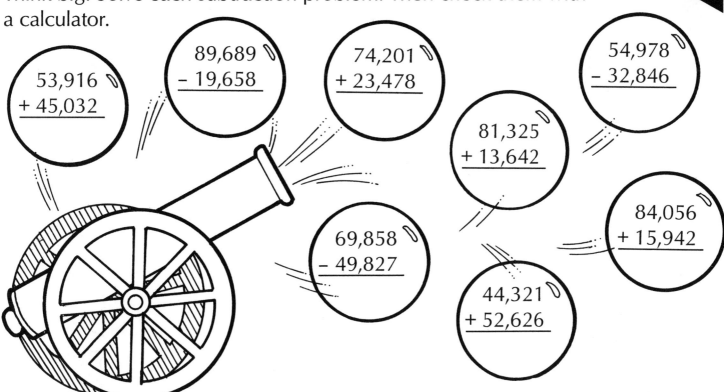

53,916
+ 45,032

89,689
− 19,658

74,201
+ 23,478

81,325
+ 13,642

54,978
− 32,846

69,858
− 49,827

44,321
+ 52,626

84,056
+ 15,942

Use a calculator to answer the question. Remember to press the equal sign after each direction.

Question: What do you get when a cannon is shot on Flag Day?

Enter: half of one thousand

x	10 tens
+	3,800
−	96
+	.618
=	↻

Answer: _____

We Salute You!

name _____

Flag Day

Solve the addition and subtraction problems.

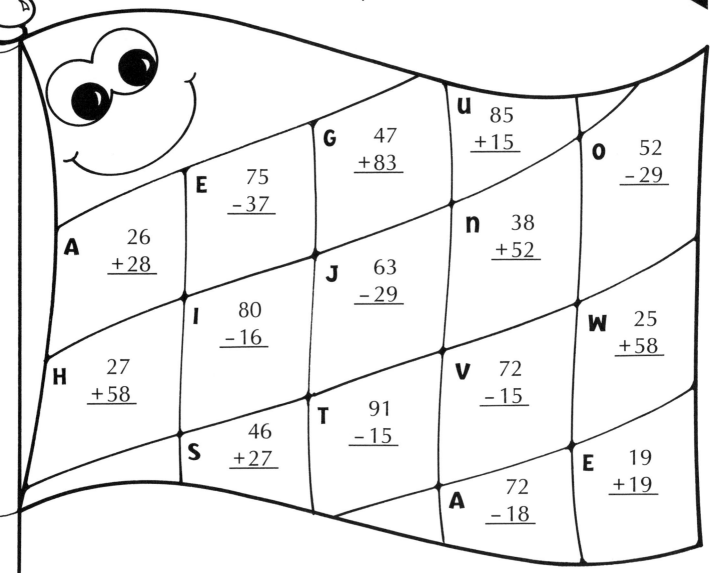

U 85
  +15

O 52
  -29

G 47
  +83

E 75
  -37

A 26
  +28

n 38
  +52

J 63
  -29

I 80
  -16

W 25
  +58

H 27
  +58

V 72
  -15

T 91
  -15

S 46
  +27

A 72
  -18

E 19
  +19

Match the letters in each box with the answers below each line to answer this question.

Proud Americans salute the U.S. flag. What does the flag do in return?

___ ___ ___ ___ ___ ___ ___ • ___ ___
90 23 76 85 64 90 130   64 76

___ ___ ___ ___ ___ ___ ___ ___ ___ •
34 100 73 76   83 54 57 38 73

Dad's "Outta This World!"

Name _____

Dad thinks his tie is very special—because it's from **you**!

Solve the problems and write the answers.

Color the space **purple** if the answer is **1–3**.

Color the space **green** if the answer is **4–6**.

Color the space **blue** if the answer is **7–9**.

Color the space **orange** if the answer is **10–12**.

Color the space **yellow** if the answer is **13–15**.

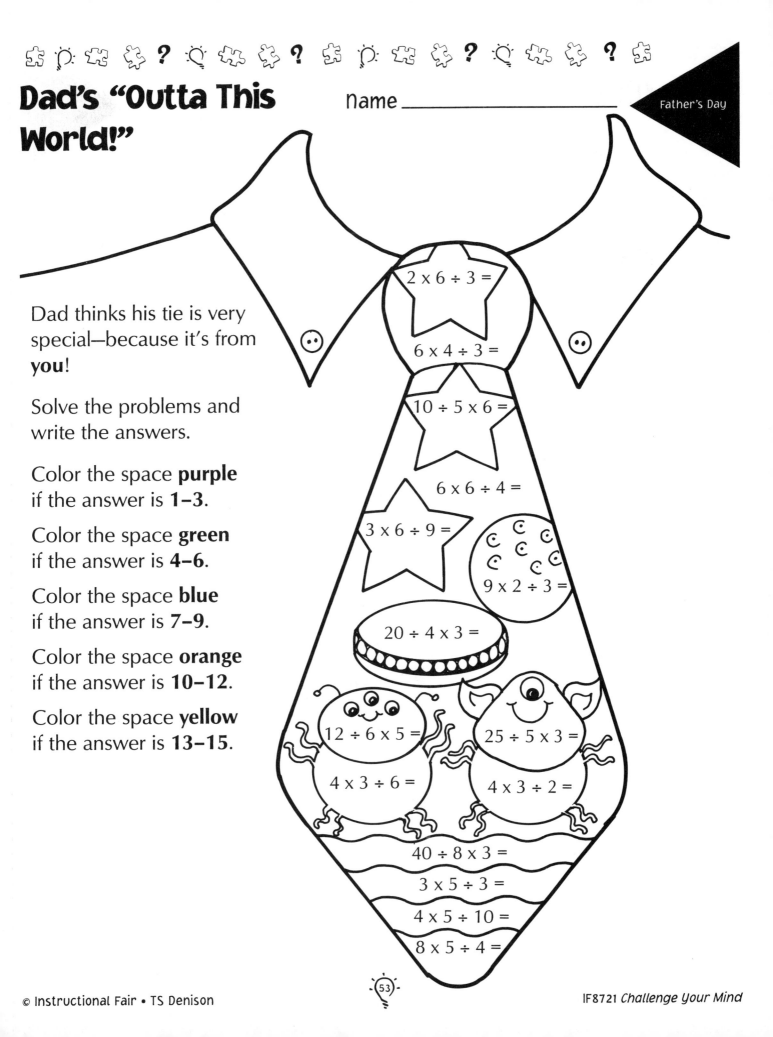

$2 \times 6 \div 3 =$

$6 \times 4 \div 3 =$

$10 \div 5 \times 6 =$

$6 \times 6 \div 4 =$

$3 \times 6 \div 9 =$

$9 \times 2 \div 3 =$

$20 \div 4 \times 3 =$

$12 \div 6 \times 5 =$

$25 \div 5 \times 3 =$

$4 \times 3 \div 6 =$

$4 \times 3 \div 2 =$

$40 \div 8 \times 3 =$

$3 \times 5 \div 3 =$

$4 \times 5 \div 10 =$

$8 \times 5 \div 4 =$

IF8721 *Challenge Your Mind*

Dear Ol' Dad

name _____

Father's Day

Use a calculator to answer the questions. Remember to press the equal key after each direction and flip the calculator at the end to read the answer.

Question: What's the main difference between a father and his young children?

Enter: half of one hundred

+	16,000
÷	five
+	5.514
=	

Answer: _____

Question: What are Dad's favorite fish to catch?

Enter: eight thousand

+	861
X	six hundred
+	eighteen
=	↻

Answer: _____

Question: What are Dad's favorite words to his child on a fishing trip?

Enter: number of cents in one dollar

+	180
÷	.05
–	1,200
+	forty-five
=	↻

Answer: _____

Question: What is a father's least favorite word from his child on a fishing trip in a boat?

Enter: number of cents in two quarters

+	7,000
–	337
x	eight
=	↻

Answer: _____

© Instructional Fair • TS Denison

54

IF8721 *Challenge Your Mind*

Superstar

Connect the dots. Start at **100** and **count by 10s**.

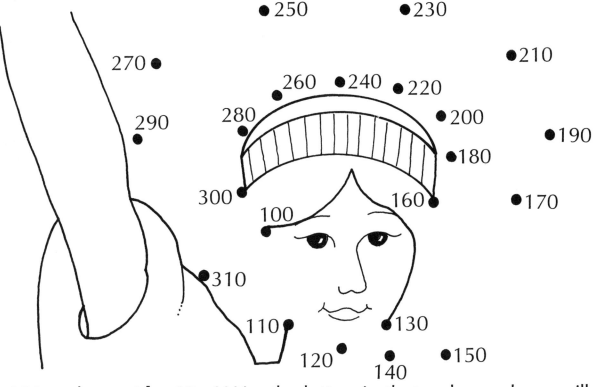

Begin at **320** and **count by 10s**. Write the letters in that order, and you will answer the question:

What should you do if the Statue of Liberty sneezes?

G	S	N	I
350	320	340	330

O	D	G
370	380	360

L	B	S	E	S
400	390	430	410	420

R	A	C	E	I	A	M
470	440	490	460	480	500	450

IF8721 *Challenge Your Mind*

Rocket's Red Glare

name _____

Solve the multiplication problems. Match the letters to the answers on the lines below.

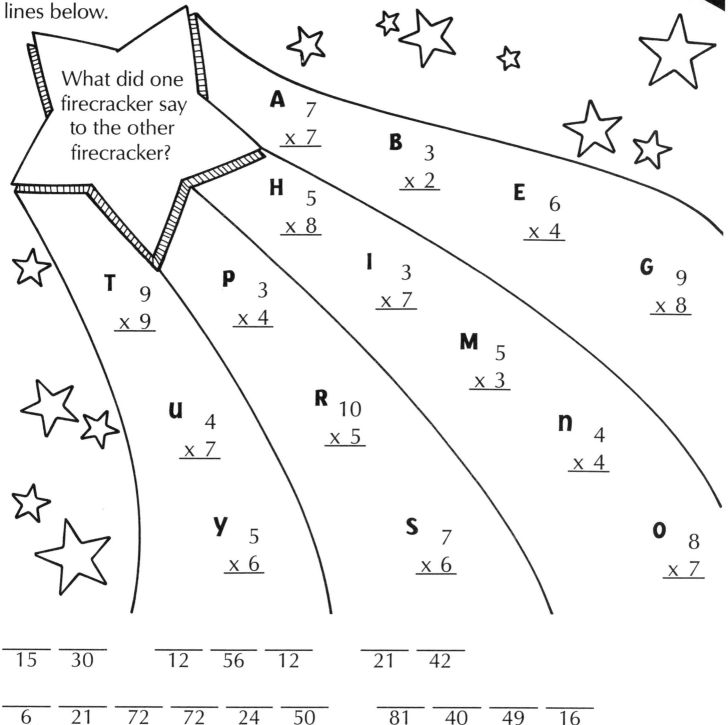

What did one firecracker say to the other firecracker?

A
7
x 7

B
3
x 2

H
5
x 8

E
6
x 4

I
3
x 7

G
9
x 8

T
9
x 9

P
3
x 4

M
5
x 3

u
4
x 7

R
10
x 5

n
4
x 4

y
5
x 6

S
7
x 6

o
8
x 7

___ ___   ___ ___ ___   ___ ___
15 30   12 56 12   21 42

___ ___ ___ ___ ___ ___   ___ ___ ___ ___
6   21 72 72 24 50   81 40 49 16

___ ___ ___ ___ ___ **!**
30 56 28 50 42

IF8721 *Challenge Your Mind*

Independence Day Parade

Name _____

Get into the spirit of the 4th of July and decorate your bike!

Color the space **red** if the number is **even**.

Color the space **blue** if the number is **odd**.

Color or leave the space **white** if the space contains no number.

© Instructional Fair • TS Denison

Say "Uncle!"

name _____

Solve the problems.

Color the space **red** if the answer is **greater than 50**.

Color the space **blue** if the answer is **between 1 and 49**.

Color or leave the space **white** if the answer is **50**.

Color the space **tan** if the answer is **0**.

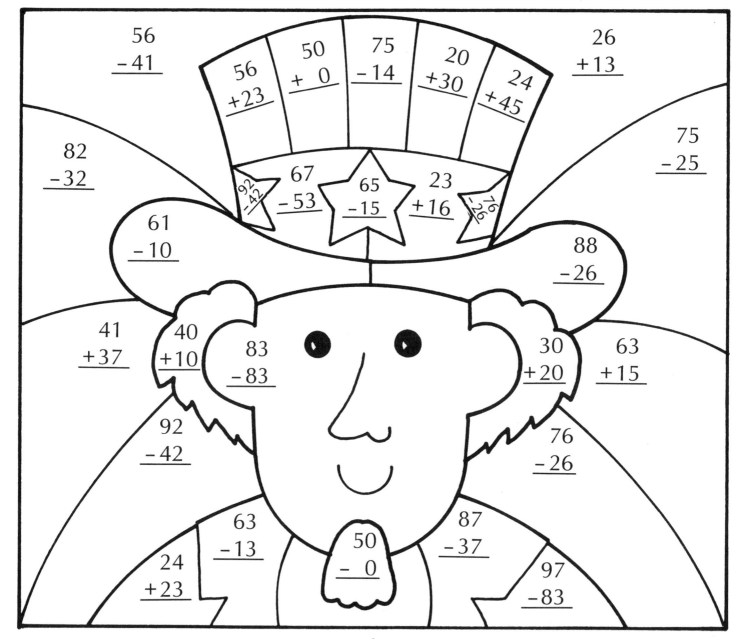

© Instructional Fair • TS Denison

IF8721 *Challenge Your Mind*

What a Dandy!

Name _____

Solve the word problems. Answer the riddle by matching the letters to the answers. Then connect the dots in order from smallest to largest.

How can you make a Yankee Doodle?

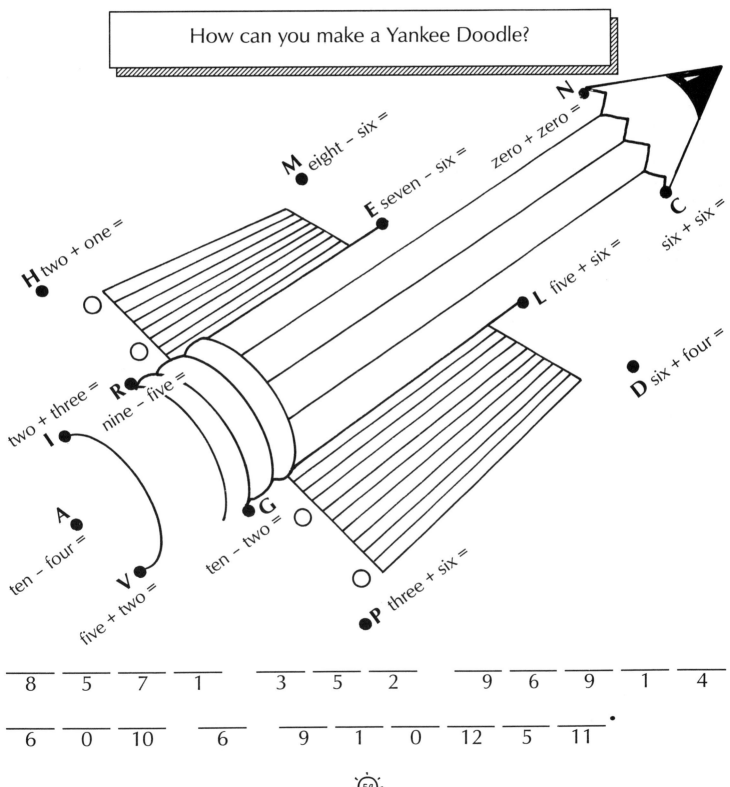

M eight – six =

E seven – six =

zero + zero =

H two + one =

L five + six =

six + six =

D six + four =

two + three =

R nine – five =

I

A ten – four =

V five + two =

G ten – two =

P three + six =

8	5	7	1		3	5	2		9	6	9	1	4

6	0	10		6		9	1	0	12	5	11	

IF8721 *Challenge Your Mind*

My Cup of Tea

name _____

Begin at **3** and count by **3s**. Write the letters in that order on the teacups, and you will answer the question:

> What was the American colonists' favorite tea?

E	Y	T	H
9	12	3	6

D	L	E	I	K
27	15	24	18	21

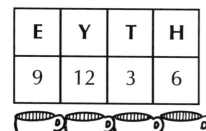

T	R	I	H	E
30	42	39	33	36

I	Y	B	L	T	E	R
48	63	51	45	60	54	57

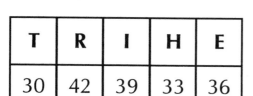

Count by **3s** and connect the dots.

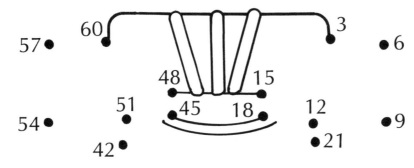

57•   60   3   •6

48   15

51   45   18   12
54•   •9
42•   •21

39•   24•
36•   •27

33•   •30

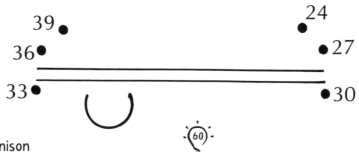

© Instructional Fair • TS Denison   60   IF8721 *Challenge Your Mind*

So Proudly We Hail

Name _____

Solve the multiplication problems. Match the letters to the answers on the lines below to solve the riddle.

> Why did Paul Revere ride his horse through town shouting, "The British are coming?"

C 25 × 1

H 52 × 3

V 91 × 6

T 71 × 2

U 42 × 4

M 85 × 1

Y 82 × 4

O 64 × 2

S 73 × 3

W 43 × 3

R 82 × 2

E 33 × 3

A 24 × 2

$\overline{142}$ $\overline{156}$ $\overline{99}$ $\overline{156}$ $\overline{128}$ $\overline{164}$ $\overline{219}$ $\overline{99}$ $\overline{129}$ $\overline{48}$ $\overline{219}$

$\overline{85}$ $\overline{168}$ $\overline{25}$ $\overline{156}$ $\overline{142}$ $\overline{128}$ $\overline{128}$ $\overline{156}$ $\overline{99}$ $\overline{48}$ $\overline{546}$ $\overline{328}$

$\overline{142}$ $\overline{128}$ $\overline{25}$ $\overline{48}$ $\overline{164}$ $\overline{164}$ $\overline{328}$.

A Loud Cry

name _____

Solve the division problems. Then match the letters and answers to the numbers on the lines below, and you will figure out the riddle.

Why did Paul Revere bring a handkerchief to Boston?

R $5\overline{)25}$

G $9\overline{)18}$

H $3\overline{)24}$

V $10\overline{)100}$

n $3\overline{)9}$

I $10\overline{)60}$

E $2\overline{)14}$

W $2\overline{)18}$

T $4\overline{)16}$

C $2\overline{)22}$

O $8\overline{)8}$

$\overline{4}$ $\overline{1}$ $\overline{2}$ $\overline{6}$ $\overline{10}$ $\overline{7}$ $\overline{4}$ $\overline{1}$ $\overline{4}$ $\overline{8}$ $\overline{7}$

$\overline{4}$ $\overline{1}$ $\overline{9}$ $\overline{3}$ $\overline{11}$ $\overline{5}$ $\overline{6}$ $\overline{7}$ $\overline{5}$

IF8721 *Challenge Your Mind*

Just a Minute, Man!

name _____

4th of July

Write the time shown on each clock. Try to do this in one minute or less while someone times you.

_____ _____ _____ _____ _____

_____ _____ _____ _____ _____

_____ _____ _____ _____ _____

How do you rate as a Minuteman?	
Number Correct	**Rank**
15	Split Secondman
13–14	Merry Minuteman
11–12	Sluggish, but Hard-Working Hourman
10 or less	Dozing Dayman

IF8721 *Challenge Your Mind*

Don't Give Up!

name _____

Circle the **smallest** number in each bottle. Use the code at the bottom of the page to write the letter on each line.

What job is very easy to stick to?

 753 735   821 830   141 137   381 390   232 321   991 919   856 685

_____ _____ _____ _____ _____ _____ _____

 322 232   919 920   106 160   685 692   871 786   463 436   216 260

_____ _____ _____ _____ _____ _____ _____

 521 529   165 106   494 501   981 987   850 821   153 137   625 619

_____ _____ _____ _____ _____ _____ _____

Code

106	494	216	521	685	232	381	786	919	821	137	981	436	735	619
A	C	E	F	G	I	K	L	N	O	R	T	U	W	Y

© Instructional Fair • TS Denison

64

IF8721 *Challenge Your Mind*

Taking It Easy

Name _____

Labor Day

Solve the number problems. Match the letters and the answers to the numbers on the lines below.

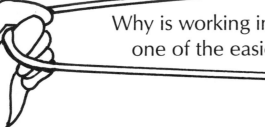

Why is working in a rubber band factory
one of the easiest jobs in the world?

A	B	C	E
56 + 9	78 − 59	67 − 29	28 + 67

H	I	n	P
45 − 18	72 + 18	83 − 15	54 + 16

S	T	u	A
66 + 14	33 − 15	59 + 19	90 − 25

,

___ ___ ___ ___ ___ ___ ___ ___ ___ ___
19   95   38   65   78   80   95   90   18   80

___ ___ ___ ___ ___ ___ ___ ___ ___ !
80   78   38   27   65   80   68   65   70

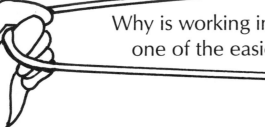

© Instructional Fair • TS Denison   65   IF8721 *Challenge Your Mind*

Fishing and Sailing

name _____

Solve each problem. Write the answer in the box.

Color the fish **red** if the answer is **1–5**.

Color the fish **yellow** if the answer is **6–10**.

Color the fish **blue** if the answer is **11–15**.

Color the fish **purple** if the answer is **16–20**.

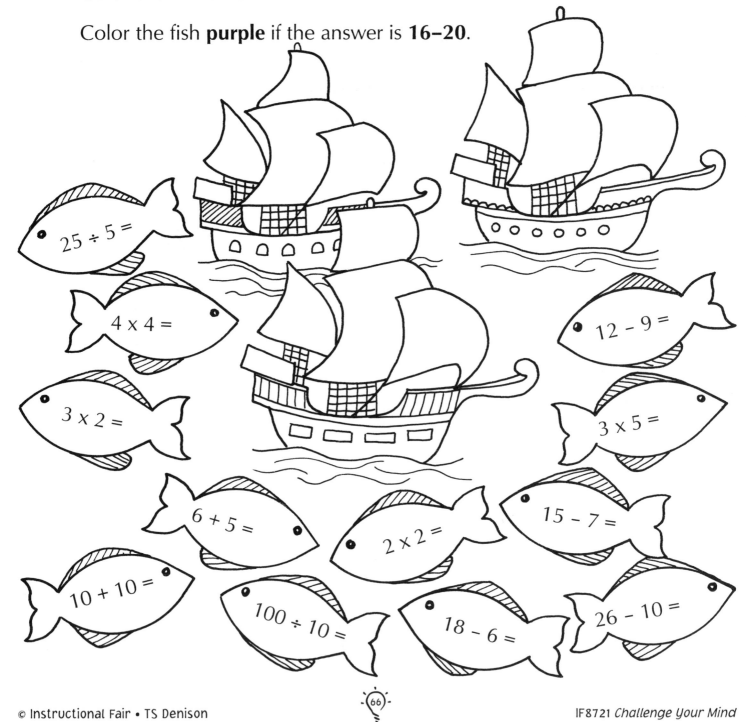

$25 \div 5 =$

$4 \times 4 =$

$12 - 9 =$

$3 \times 2 =$

$3 \times 5 =$

$6 + 5 =$

$2 \times 2 =$

$15 - 7 =$

$10 + 10 =$

$100 \div 10 =$

$18 - 6 =$

$26 - 10 =$

IF8721 *Challenge Your Mind*

Flags of the
United Nations

name _____

United Nations
Day

Color the space **orange** if the number is **1–25**.

Color the space **red** if the number is **26–50**.

Color the space **black** if the number is **51–75.**

Color the space **yellow** if the number is **76–100**.

Color the space **green** if the number is **101–125**.

Color the space **blue** if the number is **126–150**.

Color or leave the space **white** if the number is **151–175**.

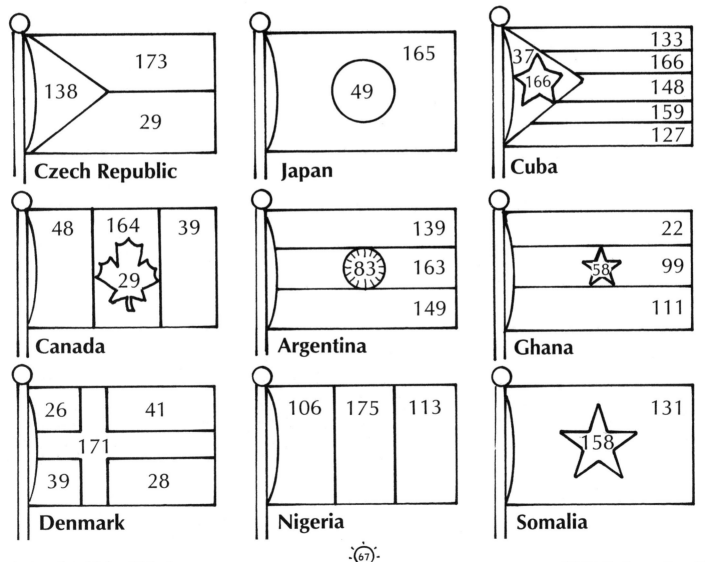

Czech Republic

Japan

Cuba

Canada

Argentina

Ghana

Denmark

Nigeria

Somalia

IF8721 *Challenge Your Mind*

Olive Branch
of Peace

Name _____

Solve each problem. Write the answers in the boxes. Then match the letters and the answers to the numbers on the lines below.

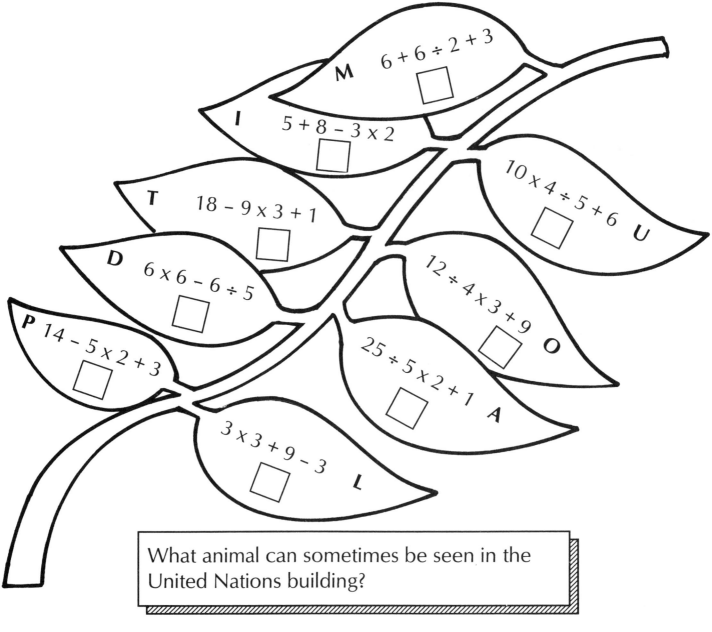

M $6 + 6 \div 2 + 3$ □

I $5 + 8 - 3 \times 2$ □

T $18 - 9 \times 3 + 1$ □

$10 \times 4 \div 5 + 6$ □ U

D $6 \times 6 - 6 \div 5$ □

$12 \div 4 \times 3 + 9$ □ O

P $14 - 5 \times 2 + 3$ □

$25 \div 5 \times 2 + 1$ □ A

$3 \times 3 + 9 - 3$ □ L

What animal can sometimes be seen in the United Nations building?

____ ____ ____ ____ ____ ____ — ____ ____ ____ ____
11   6   20 21 15 18   9   14 28 28

·💡· -68-

name _____

Each mummy is wrapped in **five** bandages marked A, B, C, D, and E. Write the two numbers on each bandage. Add them to find the length of each bandage.

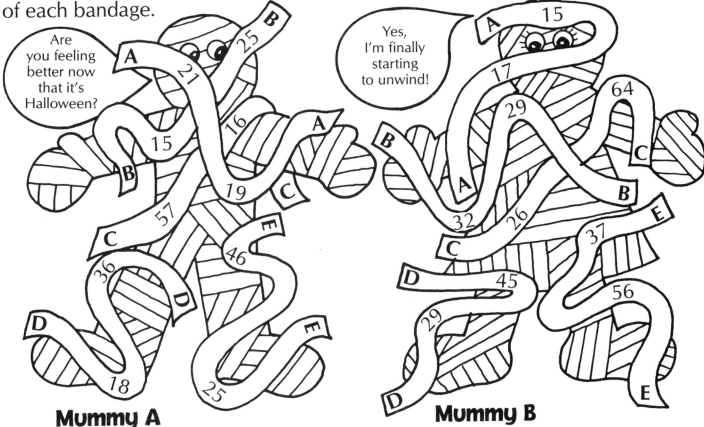

Mummy A

A ____ + ____ = ____ ft.

B ____ + ____ = ____ ft.

C ____ + ____ = ____ ft.

D ____ + ____ = ____ ft.

E ____ + ____ = ____ ft.

Mummy B

A ____ + ____ = ____ ft.

B ____ + ____ = ____ ft.

C ____ + ____ = ____ ft.

D ____ + ____ = ____ ft.

E ____ + ____ = ____ ft.

Make your mummy proud! Find which mummy is wrapped in the larger amount of bandages. Add the five sums (A, B, C, D, E) for each mummy to solve the mystery.

___ + ___ + ___ + ___ + ___ = ____ ft.   ___ + ___ + ___ + ___ + ___ = ____ ft.

A Boo-tiful Parade

name _____

Halloween

Follow the directions. Begin with the first ghost in the bottom left corner.

Directions:

1. Color a **red number 1** on the **first** ghost.

2. Draw **silly orange hats** on the **fifth** and **seventh** ghosts.

3. Color **purple polka-dots** on the **ninth** ghost.

4. Color **green stripes** on the **third** ghost.

5. Write **"Boo"** on the **tenth** ghost.

6. Draw a **big tooth** in the **second** ghost's mouth.

7. Draw **funny yellow hair** on the **fourth** ghost's head.

8. Draw **black beards** on the **sixth** and **eighth** ghosts.

© Instructional Fair • TS Denison

70

IF8721 *Challenge Your Mind*

Count on Me!

name _____

Help Igor and Agar get ready for Halloween by coloring some of their fingernails. Always begin on the left side.

Igor

AGAR

1. Count by 2s on Igor's fingers.
2. Outline those fingernails in **orange**.
3. How many are orange? _____
4. There are _____ twos in 24.
5. Write the outlined letters on the lines below.

1. Count by 3s on Agar's fingers.
2. Outline those fingernails in **black**.
3. How many are black? _____
4. There are _____ threes in 24.
5. Write the outlined letters on the lines below.

Start here.

S O M N E I L T L S T F

H I E N J G R E T R O S

E S O A N F D Y C O U O

M I U L L R K N S O W E

How does a monster count?

___ ___ ___ ___   ___ ___ ___ ___ ___

___ ___ ___ ___ ___ ___ ___ ___ ___ ___ ___

__ ___ ___ ___ ___   ___ ___ ___ ___ ___ ___ ___!

Why don't they use their feet?
(Write the remaining letters on their fingers.)

___ ___ ___ ___ ___   ___ ___ ___   ___ ___ ___ ___ ___ ___

___ ___ ___ ___   ___ ___ ___ ___   ___ ___ ___ ___ ___

___ ___ ___ ___   ___ ___ ___ ___ ___ ___!

Get the Point?

name _____

Color each character's hair and matching hat the same. You will need ten different colors.

© Instructional Fair • TS Denison

IF8721 *Challenge Your Mind*

Monster Treats

Name _____

Halloween

Frank and Stein are sorting their Halloween treats. They have already separated them into groups of the same kind. If the treats are shared equally, how many pieces of each kind will each monster get?

Circle every two treats. Write the division problem and solve it. The first one is done for you.

$8 \div 2 = 4$

Frank and Stein will each get __4__ candy bars.

Frank and Stein will each get _____ lollipops.

Frank and Stein will each get _____ pieces of taffy.

Frank and Stein will each get _____ pieces of candy corn.

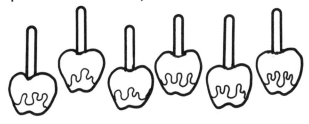

Frank and Stein will each get _____ pieces of licorice.

Frank and Stein will each get _____ caramel apples.

IF8721 *Challenge Your Mind*

Color Me Boo-tiful!

Name _____

Solve the addition problems and color each bone as directed.

34—orange	97—red	56—green
75—black	48—yellow	83—purple

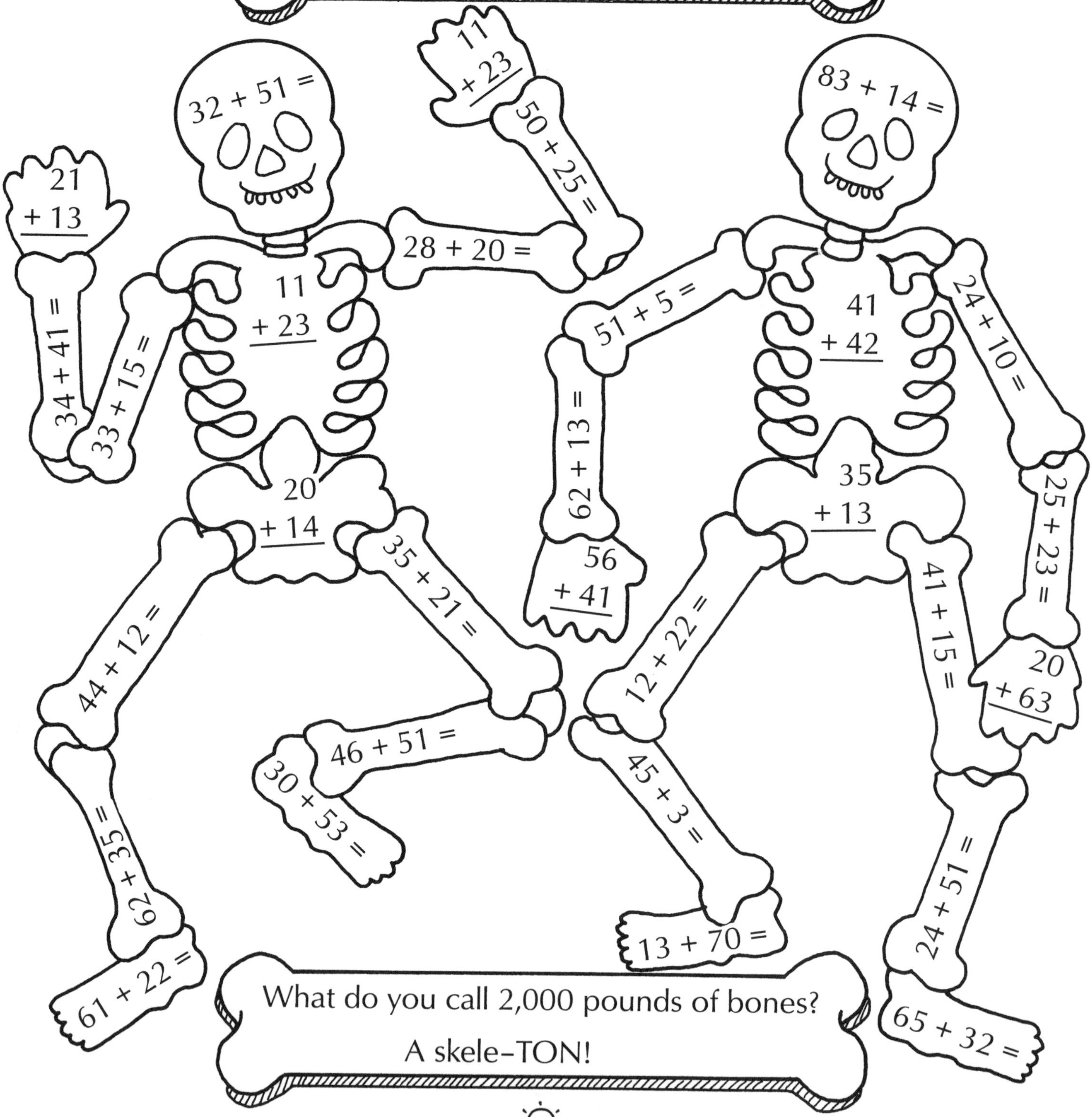

$32 + 51 =$

$11 + 23$

$83 + 14 =$

$21 + 13$

$34 + 41 =$

$33 + 15 =$

$11 + 23$

$28 + 20 =$

$50 + 25 =$

$51 + 5 =$

$41 + 42$

$24 + 10 =$

$62 + 13 =$

$56 + 41$

$25 + 23 =$

$20 + 14$

$35 + 21 =$

$35 + 13$

$41 + 15 =$

$20 + 63$

$44 + 12 =$

$46 + 51 =$

$30 + 53 =$

$12 + 22 =$

$45 + 3 =$

$24 + 51 =$

$62 + 35 =$

$61 + 22 =$

$13 + 70 =$

$65 + 32 =$

What do you call 2,000 pounds of bones?

A skele-TON!

IF8721 *Challenge Your Mind*

Watch Your Step!

name _____

Follow the directions to trace the path of each spider on its web. Stay on the lines of the web.

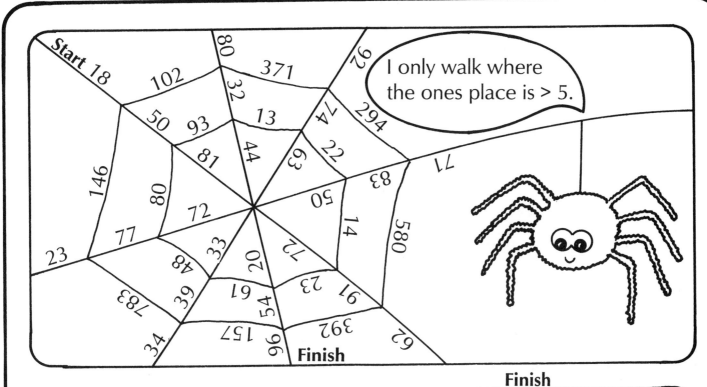

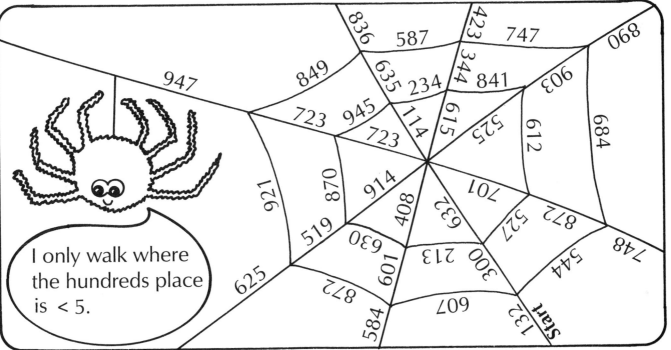

© Instructional Fair • TS Denison

IF8721 *Challenge Your Mind*

Give Me "Five!"

Name _____

Hope you have a pencil "handy." Begin at **55** and count by **5s** to connect the dots.

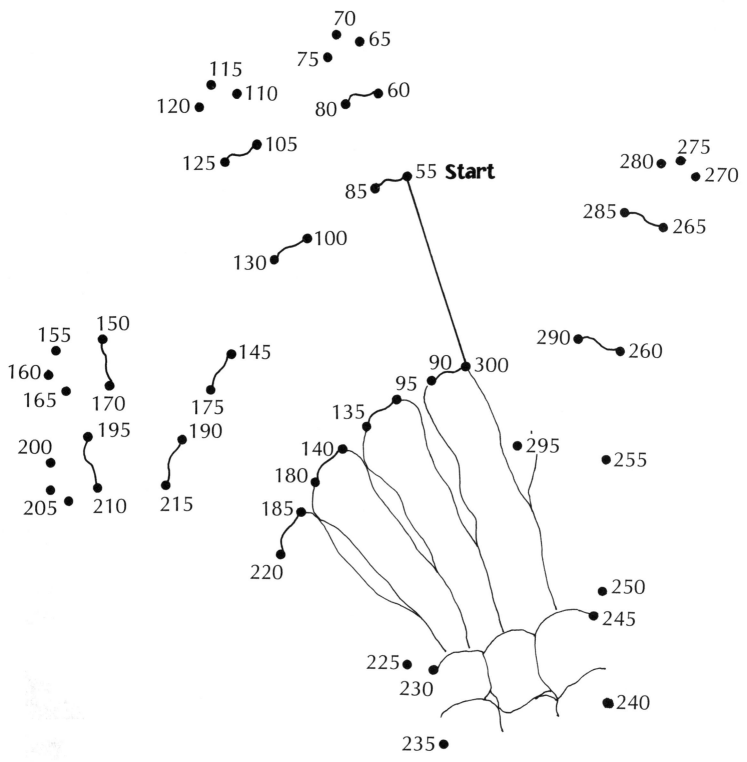

Midnight Snack

name _____

Solve the subtraction problems. Write the letters on the lines.

> What do you call a mummy who eats crackers in bed?

$\overline{26}$ $\overline{12}$ $\overline{42}$ $\overline{73}$ $\overline{11}$ $\overline{33}$ $\overline{15}$ $\overline{11}$ $\overline{43}$ $\overline{54}$ $\overline{64}$ $\overline{23}$

M	M	A	C
97 − 43	68 − 35	48 − 22	36 − 24
y	**M**	**M**	**R**
79 − 64	97 − 33	75 − 64	56 − 14
y	**u**	**M**	**u**
54 − 31	83 − 10	45 − 34	66 − 23

Glowing Grins

Name _____

Add the three numbers in each jack-o'-lantern's eyes and nose.
Write the answer in its mouth.

Color the jack-o'-lantern **orange** if the number is **even**.

Color the jack-o'-lantern **black** if the number is **odd**.

IF8721 *Challenge Your Mind*

Sailing... Sailing...

Name _____

Columbus Day

Circle the **smallest** number in each sail.

Box the **largest** number in each sail.

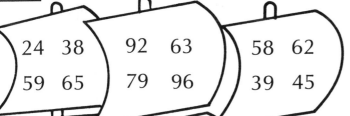

| 24 | 38 |
| 59 | 65 |

| 92 | 63 |
| 79 | 96 |

| 58 | 62 |
| 39 | 45 |

| 47 | 78 |
| 28 | 19 |

| 55 | 71 |
| 67 | 72 |

| 87 | 39 |
| 44 | 50 |

| 140 | 126 |
| 133 | 185 |

| 272 | 288 |
| 264 | 269 |

| 581 | 587 |
| 585 | 583 |

Nina

| 782 | 791 |
| 755 | 746 |

| 904 | 914 |
| 940 | 934 |

| 838 | 880 |
| 856 | 883 |

| 36 | 75 |
| 146 | 132 |

| 328 | 479 |
| 236 | 487 |

| 792 | 826 |
| 787 | 814 |

Pinta

| 527 | 461 |
| 809 | 826 |

| 401 | 324 |
| 398 | 400 |

| 940 | 904 |
| 887 | 878 |

Santa Maria

79

Birds of a Feather

name _____

Write the missing signs (+, –, =) in each feather. Use the answers and color key to color them.

3 = yellow		7 = orange	
4 = blue		8 = green	
5 = red		9 = purple	

Ticklish Situation

name _____

How many feathers does each turkey have? Read the clues and write the numbers on the lines.

This **even** number is between 380 and 390. If you add the 3 digits, the answer is 15.

I have _____ feathers.

This number is between 500 and 550. It has a 5 in the one's place. The sum of the digits is 13.

I have _____ feathers.

This **odd** number is less than 790 and more than 770. The sum of the digits is 22.

I have _____ feathers.

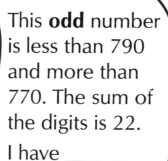

Just between us turkeys . . .

Question: What has feathers on its body, feathers under its head, and feathers floating on top of it?

Answer: A turkey sleeping on a feather pillow, snuggling under a feather comforter.

All Wrapped Up

name _____

Thanksgiving

Solve the problems by providing the missing number.

Across

2.
$$\begin{array}{r} 2 \\ \times \boxed{} \\ \hline 12 \end{array}$$

4.
$$\begin{array}{r} 39 \\ -31 \\ \hline \boxed{} \end{array}$$

7.
$$\begin{array}{r} 14 \\ +\boxed{} \\ \hline 21 \end{array}$$

8. $16 \div 4 = \boxed{}$

9.
$$\begin{array}{r} 100 \\ \times \boxed{} \\ \hline 100 \end{array}$$

Down

1. $256 = 2$ hundreds $+ \boxed{}$ tens $+ 6$ ones

3.
$$\begin{array}{r} \boxed{} \\ +73 \\ \hline 83 \end{array}$$

5. $18 \div \boxed{} = 9$

6. $83 = 8$ tens $+ \boxed{}$ ones

10. $\boxed{} \times 9 = 81$

Write the number words 1–10 in this puzzle.

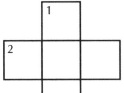

Use this code for a special message.

one	two	three	four	five	six	seven	eight	nine	ten
O	A	E	G	F	L	D	I	N	S

What did the leftover turkey drumstick say?

___ ___ ___ ___ ___ ___ ___ ___ ___ ___ ___ !
five one eight six three seven two four two eight nine

IF8721 *Challenge Your Mind*

...And the Winner Is...

name _____

Solve the problems. Then place an X on the turkey in each pair that weighs more.

IF8721 *Challenge Your Mind*

Let's Get Corny!

Name _____

Use a **yellow** crayon to circle hidden division facts (→, ↑, ↓). Write them on the lines below. One is done for you.

_____ $12 \div 6 = 2$ _____

_____ _____

_____ _____

_____ _____

_____ _____

_____ _____

IF8721 Challenge Your Mind

Please, Pass the Pumpkin Pie

Name _____

Help Grandma make **six** whole pumpkin pies by connecting the pieces that go together. Then write the letter from each piece on the line above the matching fraction below.

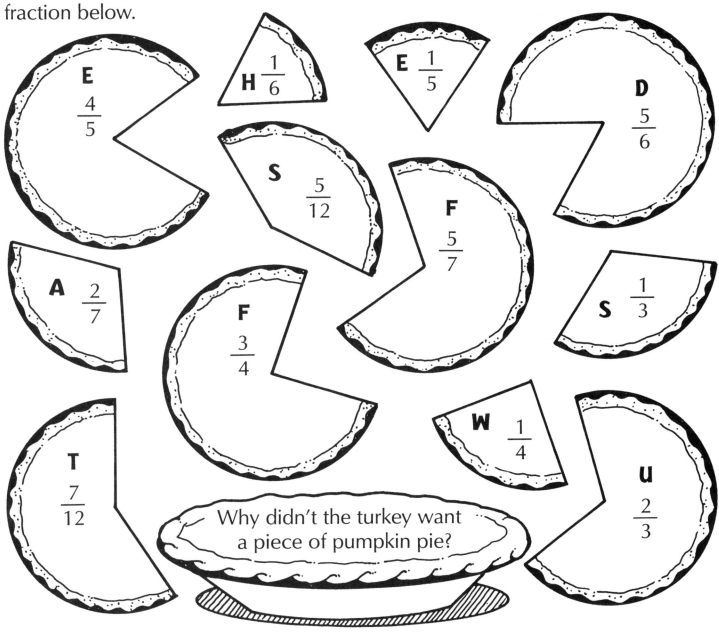

$$\frac{1}{6} \quad \frac{1}{5} \quad \frac{1}{4} \quad \frac{2}{7} \quad \frac{1}{3} \quad \frac{5}{12} \quad \frac{7}{12} \quad \frac{2}{3} \quad \frac{5}{7} \quad \frac{3}{4} \quad \frac{4}{5} \quad \frac{5}{6}$$

IF8721 *Challenge Your Mind*

Food for Thought

name _____

Solve the addition and subtraction problems. Use the code to write the letters that match the missing numbers.

Why do cranberries cry each Thanksgiving?

1	2	3	4	5	6	7	8	9	10
L	O	A	H	S	E	B	N	C	M

11	12	13	14	15	16	17	18	19	20
Y	D	T	R	P	I	B	U	C	K

```
   3        □      18       3       □       4      11
 +□      - 5      - 9     +□      - 9     +□     - 5
 ───      ───     ───     ───     ───     ───    ───
  10        1      □        6       9       9      □
 ___      ___     ___     ___     ___     ___    ___


   □        □       □      13               9      □      14     □
 -10      - 7     - 8     - 8             + 6     - 9    -□    -10
 ───      ───     ───     ───             ───     ───    ───    ───
  10        9       4      □                □       7      5      10
 ___      ___     ___     ___             ___     ___    ___    ___


   □       15               □      13       □      13
 - 2      -□              - 8     -□      + 9     - 3
 ───      ───             ───     ───     ───     ───
   0        7               5       9      15       □ !
 ___      ___             ___     ___     ___     ___
```

© Instructional Fair • TS Denison

IF8721 *Challenge Your Mind*

Anyone Home?

name _____

Cut out each triangle. Place each side of a triangle next to the side of another triangle with the answer. (**Note:** The sides that have no numbers are outside edges.) To begin, place the triangle with the sun at the top. See if you can create a tepee.

IF8721 *Challenge Your Mind*

M–M–M–MMM!

name _____

Help the Indians and Pilgrims calculate how much food to prepare for their feast. Write each answer on the line below the problem.

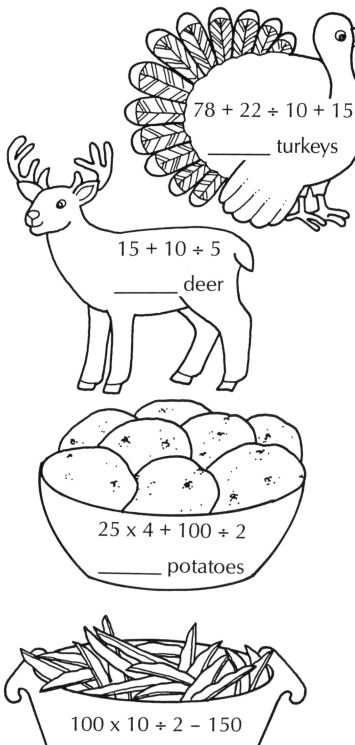

78 + 22 ÷ 10 + 15

_____ turkeys

15 + 10 ÷ 5

_____ deer

25 x 4 + 100 ÷ 2

_____ potatoes

100 x 10 ÷ 2 – 150

_____ beans

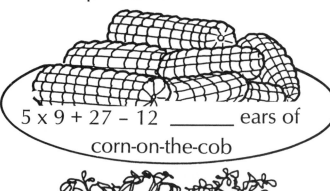

5 x 9 + 27 – 12 _____ ears of

corn-on-the-cob

75 + 55 x 2 – 100

_____ carrots

99 – 53 ÷ 2

_____ loaves of bread

20 x 5 ÷ 2 + 6

_____ apples

© Instructional Fair • TS Denison

IF8721 *Challenge Your Mind*

Stepping in the Right Direction

name _____

Look at the footsteps headed toward the Thanksgiving feast. Add <, or >, or = between each footprint. One is done for you.

26 < 92 > 75 = 75 > 35

68   78   362   91   95

21   359   83   89   257

52   52   465   475

392   392   278   342   398

405   399   410   146   138   127

826   705   692   632   632   692   701   711

700   483   64   78   53   56   53   47

© Instructional Fair • TS Denison

89

IF8721 *Challenge Your Mind*

Lighting the Mishumaa Saba

name _____

Solve the equations. Write each answer in the box.

Color the space **black** if the missing number is **0–2.**

Color the space **red** if the missing number is **3–5.**

Color the space **green** if the missing number is **6–8.**

Color the space **yellow** if the missing number is **9–11.**

Color the space **orange** if the missing number is **12–15.**

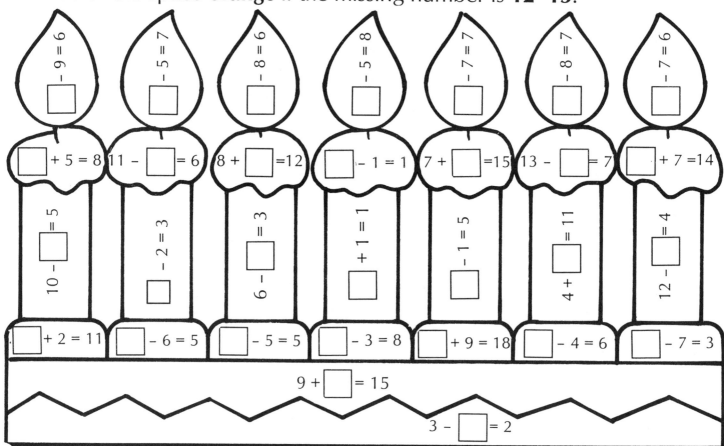

The equations on the candles:

- $- 9 = 6$
- $- 5 = 7$
- $- 8 = 6$
- $- 5 = 8$
- $- 7 = 7$
- $- 8 = 7$
- $- 7 = 6$

- $\square + 5 = 8$
- $11 - \square = 6$
- $8 + \square = 12$
- $\square - 1 = 1$
- $7 + \square = 15$
- $13 - \square = 7$
- $\square + 7 = 14$

- $10 - \square = 5$
- $\square - 2 = 3$
- $6 - \square = 3$
- $\square + 1 = 1$
- $\square - 1 = 5$
- $4 + \square = 11$
- $12 - \square = 4$

- $\square + 2 = 11$
- $\square - 6 = 5$
- $\square - 5 = 5$
- $\square - 3 = 8$
- $\square + 9 = 18$
- $\square - 4 = 6$
- $\square - 7 = 3$

- $9 + \square = 15$
- $3 - \square = 2$

Unscramble the color words.

1. The _____ candle shows the beauty of African skin.
   (cbkal)

2. The _____ candles are a reminder of past and present struggles.
   (erd)

3. The _____ candles point to a happy future.
   (ergen)

Vibunzi

name _____

Kwanzaa

Vibunzi are dried ears of corn. They represent the children in a family, who are the hope of the future.

Write the missing signs (<, >, =).

Color the kernel **red** if the sign is <.

Color the kernel **black** if the sign is >.

Color the kernel **yellow** if the sign is =.

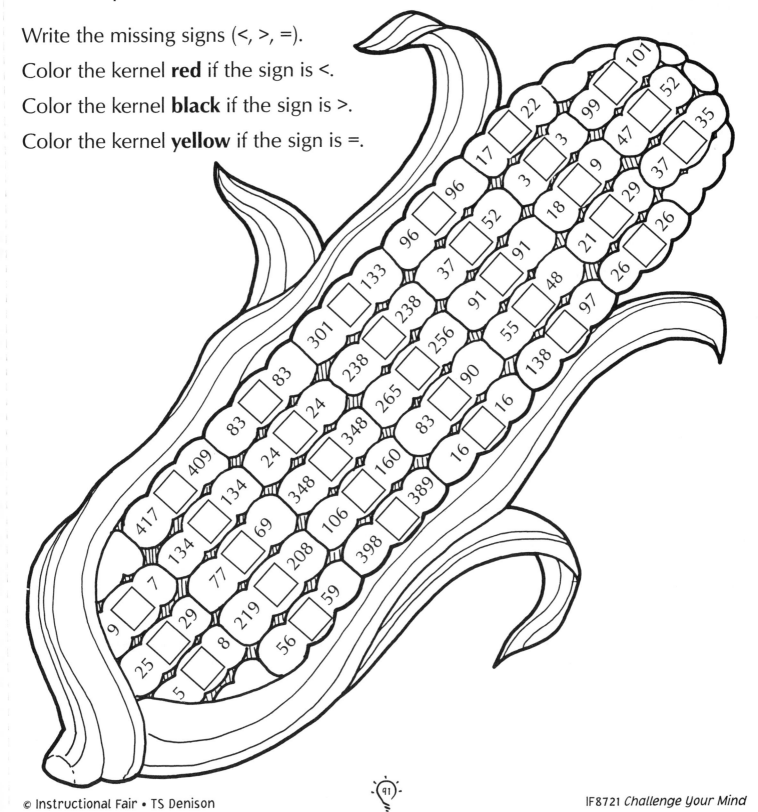

© Instructional Fair • TS Denison

IF8721 *Challenge Your Mind*

Swahili Speech

name _____

Solve each multiplication problem. Write each answer on the line. Use the code to spell Swahili words that are used during the Kwanzaa holiday. Write the letter in each box that matches the number in the code below.

9	9	4	4	6
x 3	x 4	x 4	x 9	x 6

☐ ☐ ☐ ☐ ☐
(family)

6	9	3	2	3	4
x 5	x 9	x 5	x 9	x 3	x 8

☐ ☐ ☐ ☐ ☐ ☐
(love)

4	5	2	10	3	8	12
x 5	x 3	x 4	x 2	x 8	x 2	x 3

☐ ☐ ☐ ☐ ☐ ☐ ☐
(pride)

6	9	7	6
x 8	x 4	x 7	x 4

☐ ☐ ☐ ☐
(work)

3	3	8	6	2	4
x 4	x10	x 5	x 6	x10	x 9

☐ ☐ ☐ ☐ ☐ ☐
(happiness)

3	2	6	9	4
x12	x 8	x 6	x 2	x 6

☐ ☐ ☐ ☐ ☐
(peace)

2	8	8	5	12	10	6
x 4	x 3	x 6	x 6	x 4	x 3	x 5

☐ ☐ ☐ ☐ ☐ ☐ ☐
(holiday)

4	12	2	9
x 4	x 2	x 5	x 4

☐ ☐ ☐ ☐
(tradition)

Code

A	D	E	F	H	I	J	K	L	M	N	O	P	R	S	U	Z
36	9	15	12	20	24	27	48	10	16	18	32	81	40	8	30	49

IF8721 *Challenge Your Mind*

Twelve Days of Christmas

name _____

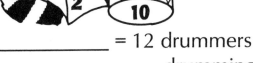
Christmas

Complete each number sentence so that the two numbers in each picture equal the number in the song. Use +, −, x, or ÷. The first number sentence is done for you.

__8 − 7__ = 1 partridge

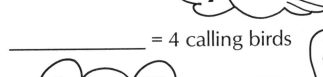

_____ = 2 turtledoves

_____ = 3 French hens

_____ = 4 calling birds

_____ = 5 golden rings

_____ = 6 geese a-laying

_____ = 7 swans a-swimming

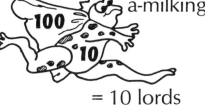

_____ = 8 maids a-milking

_____ = 9 ladies waiting

_____ = 10 lords a-leaping

_____ = 11 pipers piping

_____ = 12 drummers drumming

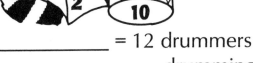

IF8721 *Challenge Your Mind*

Frosty the Snowman   name _____

Frosty the Snowman and his friends need a few items. Start at the top left and follow the directions carefully, but don't take too long or the page may melt!

1. Draw 3 coal buttons on the 1st, 3rd, 4th, and 7th snowmen.

2. Put a baseball cap on the 2nd, 5th, and 8th snowmen.

3. Wrap a big scarf around the necks of the 4th, 6th, and 10th snowmen.

4. Color orange carrot noses on the snowmen that **follow** the 3rd, 7th, and 9th snowmen.

5. Draw a coal nose on the rest of the snowmen.

6. Place a black top hat on Frosty's head. (**Hint:** He has a scarf, 3 buttons, and a carrot nose.)

Circle the **largest** number in each musical note. Use the code below to write the matching letter on the line in each note.

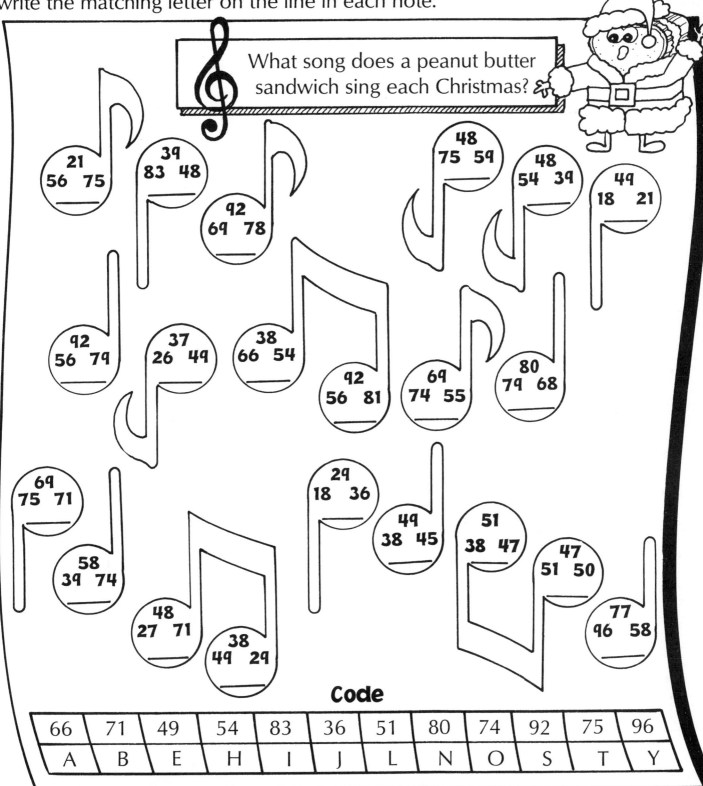

What song does a peanut butter sandwich sing each Christmas?

Code

66	71	49	54	83	36	51	80	74	92	75	96
A	B	E	H	I	J	L	N	O	S	T	Y

IF8721 *Challenge Your Mind*

Calculating Santa

name _____

(Part 1)

Use a calculator to answer the questions. Remember to press the equal key after each direction and flip the calculator at the end to read the answer.

Question: What does Santa say as he plants snow peas in his garden?

Enter: the number of pounds in 3 short tons

x	five hundred
+	40,000
+	four hundred
+	4
=	↻

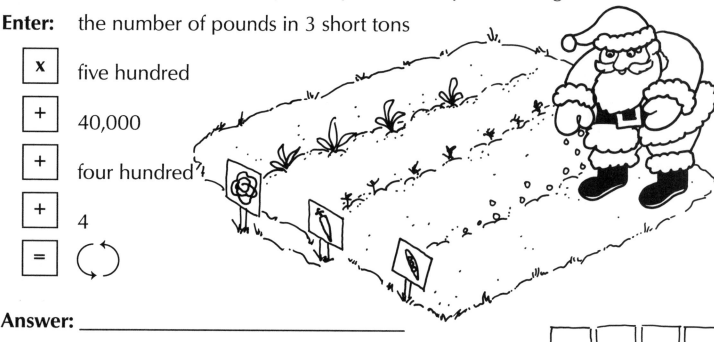

Answer: _____

Question: What does Santa call his summer home?

Enter: the number of years in a century

+	three
÷	two hundred
−	.4389
=	↻

Answer: _____

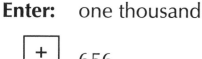

Calculating Santa
(Part 2)

name _____

Christmas

Use a calculator to answer the questions. Remember to press the equal key after each direction.

Question: How does Santa's voice change when he's getting a sore throat?

Enter: one thousand

+	656
+	.1656
÷	four thousand
=	

Answer: _____

Question: What is Santa's least favorite thing about stockings hung on a mantel?

Enter: half of 100

+	2,400
÷	.35
–	287
x	eight
=	

Answer: _____

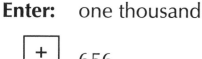

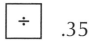

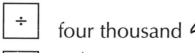

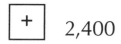

Smart Tree

name _____

Solve the subtraction problems. Match the letters to the answers to solve the riddle.

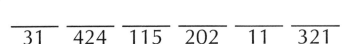

| 31 | 424 | 115 | 202 | 11 | 321 |

| 527 | 67 | 112 | 202 | 199 | 321 | 202 | 67 | 112 |

What is the name of the world's smartest Christmas tree?

A	B	E	I
156	262	325	565
−125	−147	−123	−498

L	n	P	R
878	732	655	904
−454	−620	−128	−893

S	T	E	n
395	826	468	590
−196	−505	−266	−478

While Visions of . . .   name _____

Christmas

Solve the addition problems. Write the letters on the lines.

<u>   </u> <u>   </u> <u>   </u> <u>   </u>   <u>   </u> <u>   </u> <u>   </u> <u>   </u>
912   839   639   990   839   379   469   639

<u>   </u> <u>   </u> <u>   </u> <u>   </u> <u>   </u> <u>   </u> <u>   </u>
809   699   639   836   639   889   912

<u>   </u> <u>   </u> <u>   </u> <u>   </u> <u>   </u> <u>   </u>!
983   699   639   379   904   836

How do the children all nestled in
bed sleep on Christmas eve?

A 256 +123	D 856 +127	E 364 +275	H 516 +323
M 726 +178	n 267 +622	P 482 +327	R 376 +323
S 706 +130	T 427 +485	V 275 +194	y 875 +115

IF8721 *Challenge Your Mind*

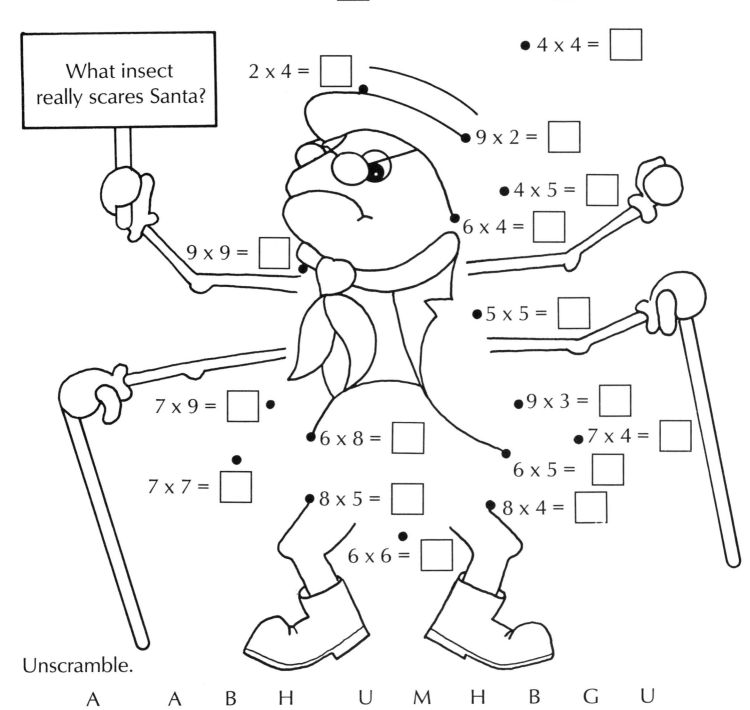

What Bugs Santa?

name _____

Christmas

Solve the multiplication problems. Then connect the answers in order from **largest** to **smallest**.

$3 \times 3 =$ ☐

$5 \times 2 =$ ☐

$4 \times 4 =$ ☐

$2 \times 4 =$ ☐

What insect really scares Santa?

$9 \times 2 =$ ☐

$4 \times 5 =$ ☐

$6 \times 4 =$ ☐

$9 \times 9 =$ ☐

$5 \times 5 =$ ☐

$7 \times 9 =$ ☐

$9 \times 3 =$ ☐

$6 \times 8 =$ ☐

$7 \times 4 =$ ☐

$7 \times 7 =$ ☐

$6 \times 5 =$ ☐

$8 \times 5 =$ ☐

$8 \times 4 =$ ☐

$6 \times 6 =$ ☐

Unscramble.

A   A   B   H   U   M   H   B   G   U

___ ___ ___ ___ ___ ___ ___ ___ ___ ___

IF8721 *Challenge Your Mind*

Trip up North

name _____

Christmas

Find the safest way to travel to the North Pole. Follow the clues to connect the dots. Be careful! Not all numbers will be used.

Clues

1. 6 tens = _____

2. The number in the hundreds place in 849 _____

3. 900 + 50 + 6 = 9 _____ 6

4. 7 hundreds = _____

5. The number in the tens place in 934 _____

6. 400 + 60 + 1 = 46_____

7. 2 ones = _____

8. 2 hundreds + 9 tens + 5 ones = 200 + _____ + 5

● 90

2
●

● 200

10 ●

● 1

● 9

● 3

700 ●

● 8

● 6

●
70

● 5

● 60

Start
●

© Instructional Fair • TS Denison

IF8721 *Challenge Your Mind*

A Special Glow

name _____

Find the missing part of each candle to make it whole. Color it the same color as the part shown in the **menorah** (candle holder).

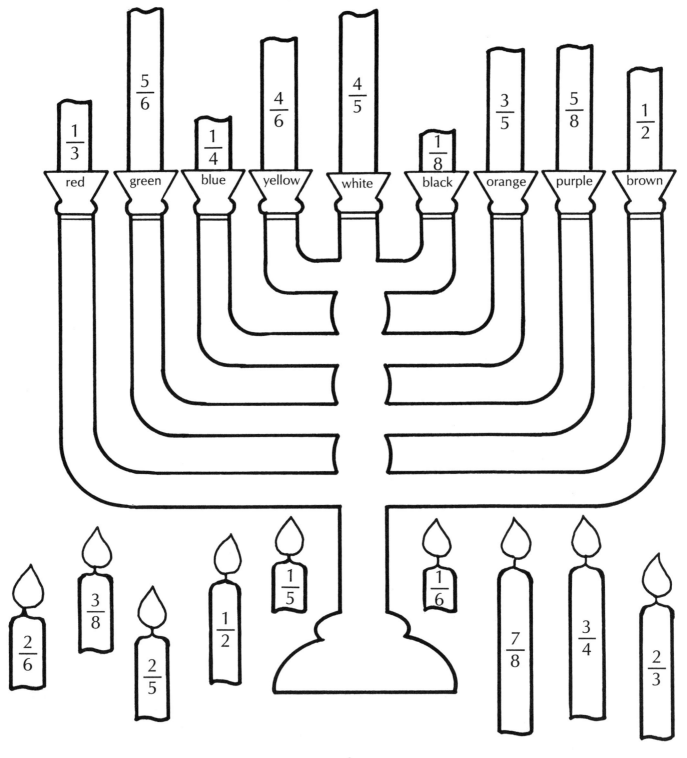

© Instructional Fair • TS Denison

IF8721 *Challenge Your Mind*

Take a Spin

name _____

Hanukkah

"I'll spin the dreidel, and I'll see,
What stays in the pot and what's left for me!"

Read the definition of each dreidel symbol. Then study each game and fill in the missing blanks.

Dreidel Symbols		
נ =	Nun (none):	Player takes nothing.
ג =	Gimmel (give):	Player takes everything in the pot. All players then add one more object to the pot.
ה =	Heh (half):	Player takes half of the pot. If there's an odd number in the pot, the player takes the larger half.
ש =	Shin (add):	Player adds one object to the pot.

Game 1

Four children are playing dreidel with pieces of candy. Thirty pieces remain in the pot. It is Isaac's turn. He spins ה and receives ____ piece(s) of candy. That leaves ____ piece(s) in the pot.

Next, Hannah spins ש . She must add ____ piece(s) to the pot. Now the pot has ____ piece(s) of candy.

Tommy takes his turn, and the dreidel shows ה . He gets ____ piece(s) of candy while ____ piece(s) remain in the pot.

Then Susie spins ג . She takes ____ piece(s) of candy. The number of pieces in the pot has changed to _____ , until each child adds one piece making the pot contain ____ piece(s).

Game 2

Mark, Kathy, and Bernie are using bottle caps in their dreidel game. At this point the pot has 23 bottle caps.

Mark frowns after he spins נ because he receives ____ bottle cap(s) while the pot has ____ . Then Kathy spins ה . Because she gets the larger half, she takes ____ bottle cap(s) and leaves ____ in the pot. Bernie spins ש . This changes the number of bottle caps in the pot to ____ .

IF8721 *Challenge Your Mind*

It All Begins in January

Name _____

Use the Word Bank to complete this calendar page.

January

Sun.	Mon.	Tues.	Wed.	Thurs.	Fri.	Sat.
				one	two	three
four A	five	six B	seven C	eight	nine	ten D
eleven E	twelve I	thirteen	fourteen M	fifteen N	sixteen	seventeen
eighteen	nineteen R	twenty	twenty- one S	twenty- two T	twenty- three	twenty- four
twenty- five U	twenty- six	twenty- seven	twenty- eight Y	twenty- nine	thirty	thirty- one

Word Bank
eight
eleven
fifteen
five
four
nineteen
fourteen
one
seven
six
ten
twelve
two

Now use the number words on the calendar to write the letters that answer the riddle.

Why does a calendar feel sad on New Year's Eve?

B E C A U S E   I T S
6 11 7 4 25 21   12 22 21

D A Y S   A R E
10 4 28 21   4 19 11

N U M B E R E D !
15 25 14 6 11 19 11 10

Page 4

Countdown

Name _____

It's getting close to midnight!

Color the clock **yellow** if there are 50–55 minutes before midnight.

Color the clock **blue** if there are 35–45 minutes before midnight.

Color the clock **green** if there are 20–30 minutes before midnight.

Color the clock **red** if there are 5–15 minutes before midnight.

Color the clock **purple** if it is **midnight**.

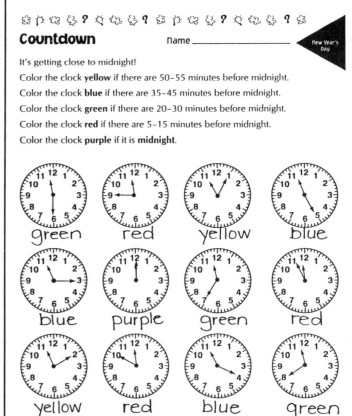

green   red   yellow   blue

blue   purple   green   red

yellow   red   blue   green

Page 5

Peace March

Name _____

Martin Luther King, Jr., was born on January 15, 1929. In 1963, Dr. King led over 250,000 people to the Lincoln Memorial and spoke of living together in peace.

Mark the marcher's path by coloring all footsteps that equal 15.

Page 6

We Go Together

Name _____

Can you find the missing fact from each family?

H
6 + 2 = 8
8 − 6 = 2
2 + 6 = 8

F
9 − 4 = 5
4 + 5 = 9
9 − 5 = 4

M
7 + 3 = 10
10 − 3 = 7
10 − 7 = 3

K
1 + 5 = 6
6 − 5 = 1
5 + 1 = 6

I
8 − 3 = 5
3 + 5 = 8
5 + 3 = 8

E
10 − 6 = 4
4 + 6 = 10
10 − 4 = 6

W
4 + 7 = 11
11 − 7 = 4
11 − 4 = 7

R
12 − 9 = 3
3 + 9 = 12
12 − 3 = 9

S
4 + 3 = 7
7 − 3 = 4
3 + 4 = 7

O
5 + 6 = 11
11 − 6 = 5
6 + 5 = 11

L
2 + 8 = 10
10 − 8 = 2
10 − 2 = 8

C
9 + 4 = 13
13 − 9 = 4
4 + 9 = 13

X
6 + 8 = 14
8 + 6 = 14
14 − 8 = 6

To solve the riddle write the letter on the groundhog's shadow that matches the missing fact.

What do you get when you cross a groundhog with your principal?

S I X   M O R E
7−4=3 8−5=3 14−6=8   3+7=10 11−5=6 9+3=12 6+4=10

W E E K S   O F
7+4=11 6+4=10 6+4=10 6+1=5 7−4=3   11−5=6 5+4=9

S C H O O L
7−4=3 13−4=9 8−2=6 11−5=6 11−5=6 8+2=10

Page 7

Armloads of Valentines

Name _____

Valentine's Day

Connect the dots by counting from 50 to 100. Who has lots of valentines to deliver?

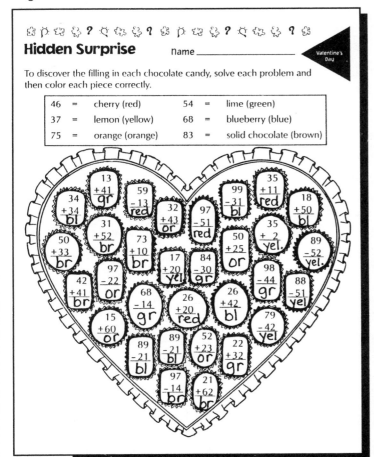

Page 8

Heart to Heart

Name _____

Valentine's Day

Recopy each group of hearts in order from smallest to largest to answer each riddle. Write both the numbers and the words.

What happened to the Valentine sweethearts who wanted to kiss in the fog?

They — tried — but — they — mist.
349 — 361 — 441 — 482 — 501

How do you kiss a hockey player?

You — need — to — pucker — up.
158 — 179 — 190 — 217 — 270

What did the postage stamp say to the envelope on Valentine's Day?

I — am — stuck — on — you.
87 — 96 — 101 — 110 — 115

What did the snake say to his special sweetie?

Give — me — a — little — hiss
23 — 37 — 41 — 54 — 58

Page 9

Hidden Surprise

Name _____

Valentine's Day

To discover the filling in each chocolate candy, solve each problem and then color each piece correctly.

46	=	cherry (red)	54	=	lime (green)
37	=	lemon (yellow)	68	=	blueberry (blue)
75	=	orange (orange)	83	=	solid chocolate (brown)

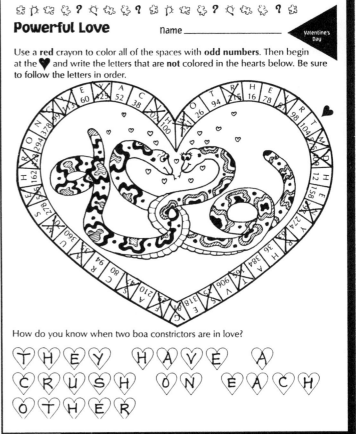

Page 10

Powerful Love

Name _____

Valentine's Day

Use a **red** crayon to color all of the spaces with **odd numbers**. Then begin at the 💜 and write the letters that are **not** colored in the hearts below. Be sure to follow the letters in order.

How do you know when two boa constrictors are in love?

T H E Y ♥ H A V E ♥ A
C R U S H ♥ O N ♥ E A C H
O T H E R

Page 11

IF8721 *Challenge Your Mind*

Love Pranks

Name _____

Valentine's Day

Cupid has been busy shooting his love arrows. Add the numbers in the hearts. Then, draw lines to the hearts that match to discover who Cupid's arrows hit.

Page 12

Royal Tarts

Name _____

Valentine's Day

Follow each path from the Queen of Hearts to her royal cousins. Discover how many tarts she made for each of them for Valentine's Day. Write that number on their crowns.

Page 13

Mending Broken Hearts

Name _____

Valentine's Day

Mend the broken hearts by coloring the matching halves the same color. You will need **six** different colors.

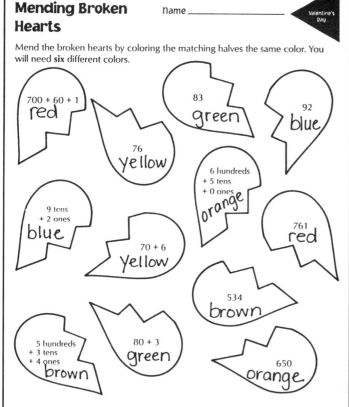

700 + 60 + 1 red
83 green
92 blue
76 yellow
6 hundreds + 5 tens + 0 ones orange
9 tens + 2 ones blue
70 + 6 yellow
761 red
534 brown
5 hundreds + 3 tens + 4 ones brown
80 + 3 green
650 orange

Page 14

Presidential Humor

Name _____

Presidents Day

Solve the subtraction problems. Match the letters to the answers beneath each line to find out which president had the most children.

A	B	C	E
18 − 9 = 9	6 − 6 = 0	10 − 2 = 8	8 − 7 = 1
F	**G**	**H**	**I**
11 − 9 = 2	15 − 9 = 6	12 − 9 = 3	10 − 5 = 5
N	**O**	**R**	**S**
14 − 7 = 7	9 − 5 = 4	20 − 10 = 10	16 − 3 = 13
T	**U**	**W**	**Y**
14 − 2 = 12	15 − 0 = 15	18 − 7 = 11	16 − 2 = 14

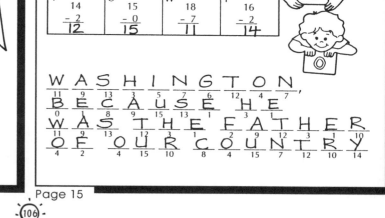

W A S H I N G T O N ,
11 9 13 3 5 7 6 12 4 7

B E C A U S E   H E
0 1 8 9 15 13 1 3 1

W A S   T H E   F A T H E R
11 9 13 12 3 1 2 9 12 3 1 7

O F   O U R   C O U N T R Y
4 2 4 15 10 8 4 15 7 12 10 14

Page 15

© Instructional Fair • TS Denison

IF8721 *Challenge Your Mind*

Color Me Lucky
Name _____

St. Patrick's Day

Solve each problem and write the answer next to it.

If the number is < 20, color it **green**.

If the number is = 20, color it **orange**.

If the number is > 20, color it **tan**.

Lucky numbers
Name _____

St. Patrick's Day

This leprechaun's lucky number is 9.

Color the shamrock **green** if the 9 is in the **hundreds place**.

Color the shamrock **yellow** if the 9 is in the **tens place**.

Color the shamrock **orange** if the 9 is in the **ones place**.

Find and circle the leprechaun's very lucky shamrock. If you add all three digits of this shamrock together, you will get nine.

Golden names
Name _____

St. Patrick's Day

Write and solve the number problems by matching the letters in each name with the correct number.

If a leprechaun's name indicates his worth in gold, how many coins of gold is each leprechaun worth? Then color the leprechaun whose name is worth the most.

A	I	E	L	N	O	D	S	T	Y	U	R
1	2	3	4	5	6	7	8	9	10	11	12

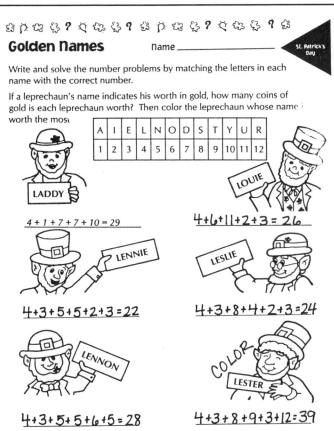

LADDY

$4 + 1 + 7 + 7 + 10 = 29$

LOUIE

$4 + 6 + 11 + 2 + 3 = 26$

LENNIE

$4 + 3 + 5 + 5 + 2 + 3 = 22$

LESLIE

$4 + 3 + 8 + 4 + 2 + 3 = 24$

LENNON

$4 + 3 + 5 + 5 + 6 + 5 = 28$

LESTER

$4 + 3 + 8 + 9 + 3 + 12 = 39$

Pure Gold
Name _____

St. Patrick's Day

Help the leprechaun sort his genuine gold coins from the fake ones. Color the coin **golden** (yellow) if the number on it is **even**. Color the coin **brown** if the number is **odd**.

Page 16

Page 17

Page 18

Page 19

© Instructional Fair • TS Denison

IF8721 *Challenge Your Mind*

How many coins does each leprechaun have in his pot? Read the clues and write the number on the pot.

The number of my coins is an even number. It is greater than 50 and less than 62. The sum of its two digits is 13.

58

My coins are a factor of 5. I have less than 60 coins. The sum of its two digits is 10.

55

I'm glad I have 3 more coins than the second highest leprechaun.

77

I have saved an odd number of coins. It is half of 100 plus 17.

67

I've collected more than 65 coins but less than 75. The sum of its two digits is 11. The first digit is larger than the second.

74

Begin at **50** and count by **10s**. Write the corresponding letters in that order in the shamrocks to answer this question:

What would happen if a leprechaun jogged into a field of four-leaf clovers?

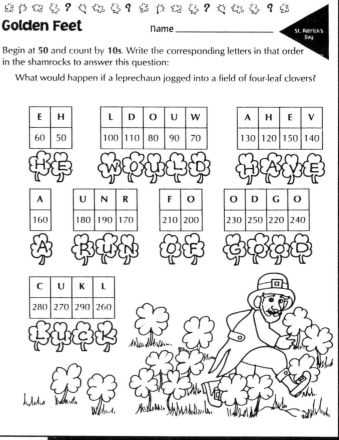

E	H
60	50

L	D	O	U	W
100	110	80	90	70

A	H	E	V
130	120	150	140

HE WOULD HAVE

A
160

U	N	R
180	190	170

F	O
210	200

O	D	G	O
230	250	220	240

A RUN OF GOOD

C	U	K	L
280	270	290	260

LUCK

Help the leprechaun climb over the rainbow to reach his pot of gold. Solve each addition problem. Then look at the first three boxes in a row. Which one equals 2? Color it any color. Climb to the next three boxes. Which one equals 4? Color it another color. Continue counting by 2s until you reach the pot of gold. Try to use a different color for each row.

Each whole pot of gold contains $1.00. Count the money in each half and write the amount on the pot. Then draw a line to connect the two halves that equal $1.00.

Page 20

Page 21

Page 22

Page 23

IF8721 *Challenge Your Mind*

Easter Mix-Up

Name _____

Easter

Find out what you get . . .
   when you cross a baby Easter chick and a baby Easter bunny.

Cut out the squares at the bottom of this page and paste them onto the boxes with the same number. (Bold lines show the top of the square.)

1 one	2 two	3 three	4 four	5 five
6 six	7 seven	8 eight	9 nine	10 ten
11 eleven	12 twelve	13 thirteen	14 fourteen	15 fifteen

seven   fourteen   ten   eight   three

thirteen   five   twelve   one   fifteen

two   eleven   four   nine   six

Page 24

It's a Draw!

Name _____

Easter

A **line of symmetry** shows that one half will be exactly the same as the other half.

Finish drawing these pictures by making both halves the same. Use the grid lines as a guide.

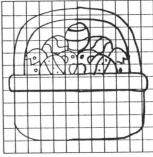

Page 25

Mystery Eggs

Name _____

Easter

Write the missing numbers in each mystery egg. Multiply the numbers both down (↓) and across (→) and get the third number as a product.

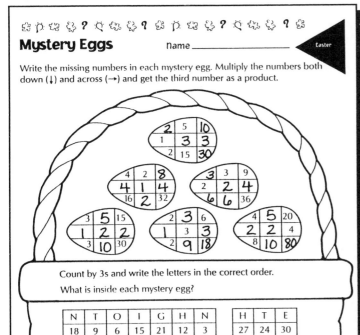

Count by 3s and write the letters in the correct order.

What is inside each mystery egg?

N	T	O	I	G	H	N		H	T	E
18	9	6	15	21	12	3		27	24	30

N O T H I N G .   T H E

L	O	Y	K		S	I	N		N	O		U	Y	O
39	36	33	42		48	45			54	51		63	57	60

Y O L K   I S   O N   Y O U !

Page 26

Duck . . . Duck . . . Chick!

Name _____

Easter

Draw a line from a duck in the first column to a duck in the second column to a chick in the third column to form a division sentence. Use a different color for each problem.

Page 27

"Eggstra" Big Eggs   Name _____

Put the eggs in order from largest to smallest. Write the numbers on the eggs below each basket.

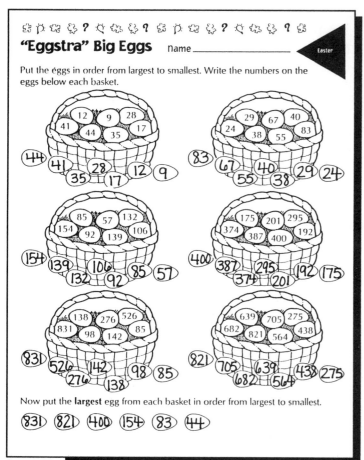

Now put the **largest** egg from each basket in order from largest to smallest.

(831) (821) (400) (154) (83) (44)

Dozen It Make Sense?   Name _____

Read each clue. Then color eggs in each carton as directed.

3 blue eggs.   2 yellow eggs.
All of the rest are green and pink.
There is 1 more pink egg than green.

B B B Y Y G
G G P P P P

2 purple eggs.
There are twice as many green eggs as purple.
There are 3 times as many yellow eggs as purple.

P G G Y Y Y
P G G Y Y Y

3 pink eggs
There is 1 more yellow egg than pink. There is one more orange egg than yellow.

P P P Y Y Y
Y O O O O O

There are the same number of blue and green eggs.
2 purple eggs.

B B B B B P
G G G G G P

4 times as many yellow eggs as green,
4 blue eggs.
1 less purple egg than blue.

B B P P Y Y
B B P G Y Y

3 red eggs.
There are twice as many blue eggs as red.
There are half as many yellow eggs as blue.

R R R Y Y Y
B B B B B B

Page 29

Joking Around   Name _____

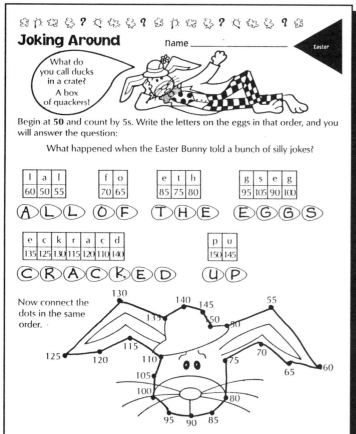

What do you call ducks in a crate? A box of quackers!

Begin at **50** and count by 5s. Write the letters on the eggs in that order, and you will answer the question:

What happened when the Easter Bunny told a bunch of silly jokes?

| l | a | l | | f | o | | e | t | h | | g | s | e | g |
|60|50|55| |70|65| |85|75|80| |95|105|90|100|

A L L   O F   T H E   E G G S

| e | c | k | r | a | c | d | | p | u |
|135|125|130|115|120|110|140| |150|145|

C R A C K E D   U P

Now connect the dots in the same order.

Page 30

Quadruplets   Name _____

Solve each problem. Write the answer on the jellybean. Find each set of **four** jellybeans whose answers are equal and color them the same color. You will need **six** different colors.

Page 31

© Instructional Fair • TS Denison

110

IF8721 *Challenge Your Mind*

Cracked Eggs

Name _____

Easter

Match the two pieces of eggs that have equal sums by coloring each half the same color. You will need eight different colors.

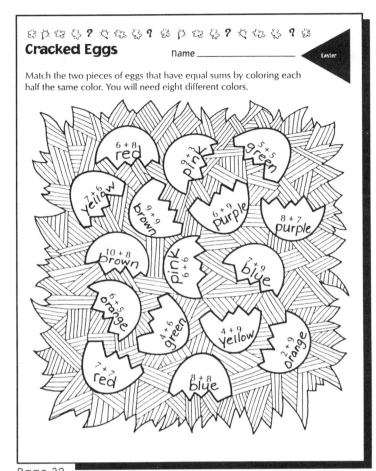

Page 32

Coloring Easter Eggs

Name _____

Easter

Solve each multiplication fact. Then color the picture by matching the answers with the colors.

orange	yellow	red	green
9 × 3 = 27	6 × 6 = 36	8 × 8 = 64	2 × 8 = 16
5 × 2 = 10	6 × 4 = 24	5 × 5 = 25	4 × 3 = 12	9 × 9 = 81	7 × 3 = 21	4 × 8 = 32	10 × 10 = 100

brown	purple	white	blue
8 × 7 = 56	5 × 9 = 45	2 × 7 = 14	4 × 5 = 20
9 × 0 = 0	7 × 4 = 28	3 × 3 = 9	6 × 8 = 48	6 × 3 = 18	5 × 8 = 40	8 × 9 = 72	6 × 7 = 42

Page 33

Jellybean Countdown

Name _____

Easter

Read the clues and write the number of jellybeans on each line. Color the basket of jellybeans when you have answered the number riddles.

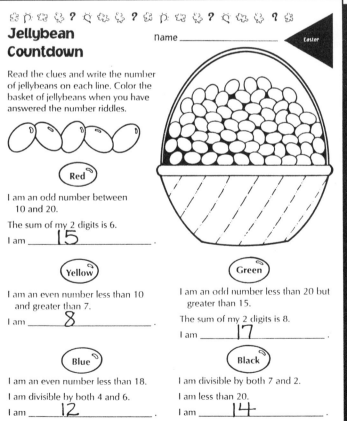

Red

I am an odd number between 10 and 20.

The sum of my 2 digits is 6.

I am ___15___ .

Yellow

I am an even number less than 10 and greater than 7.

I am ___8___ .

Blue

I am an even number less than 18.

I am divisible by both 4 and 6.

I am ___12___ .

Green

I am an odd number less than 20 but greater than 15.

The sum of my 2 digits is 8.

I am ___17___ .

Black

I am divisible by both 7 and 2.

I am less than 20.

I am ___14___ .

Page 34

Special Dinner

Name _____

April Fool's Day

"Billy, why is my spaghetti moving?" asked little sister Tonya.

"I don't know what you mean," snickered Billy.

Use your noodle. Add all **six** numbers on each worm and write your answer on its head. (**Hint:** All of the numbers on each worm are different.)

Page 35

© Instructional Fair • TS Denison

IF8721 *Challenge Your Mind*

No Business like Shoe Business

Name _____

April Fool's Day

Oh, no! A prankster took everyone's tennis shoes and threw them into a big pile. Now they need to be arranged in pairs. Each pair of shoes contains a pair of **consecutive numbers** (like 256, 257 or 921, 922). Write the numbers for each pair on the lines below.

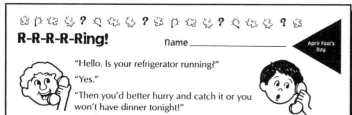

823, 824   434, 435   637, 638
874, 875   382, 383   385, 386
959, 960   579, 580   763, 764
837, 838

Real Cut-Ups

Name _____

April Fool's Day

This is confusing! Someone cut flash cards in half. Put them back together by writing each addition or subtraction fact on the blank cards below.

$$\begin{array}{r}4\\+7\\\hline 11\end{array}\quad\begin{array}{r}5\\+8\\\hline 13\end{array}\quad\begin{array}{r}9\\-3\\\hline 6\end{array}\quad\begin{array}{r}7\\-2\\\hline 5\end{array}\quad\begin{array}{r}3\\+9\\\hline 12\end{array}\quad\begin{array}{r}8\\-2\\\hline 6\end{array}$$

R-R-R-R-Ring!

Name _____

April Fool's Day

"Hello. Is your refrigerator running?"

"Yes."

"Then you'd better hurry and catch it or you won't have dinner tonight!"

Stop the refrigerator by finding the mistake it made while running away. Color that space **red**.

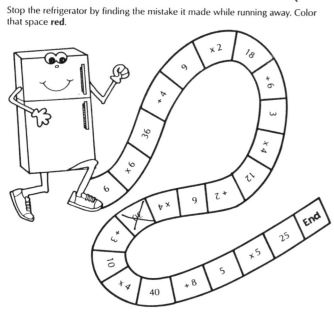

Yuk!

Name _____

April Fool's Day

Begin at **68** and count backwards by 2s. Write the letters in that order on the bugs, and you will answer the question:

What has two heads, twenty-four legs, and sharp, pointy teeth?

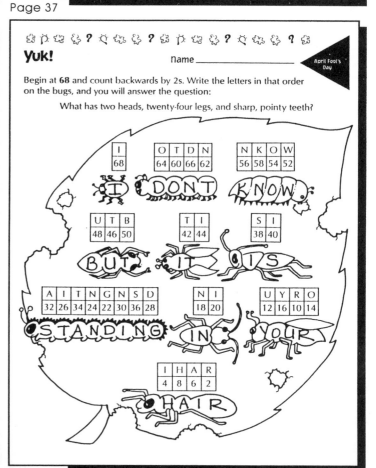

© Instructional Fair • TS Denison

112

IF8721 *Challenge Your Mind*

Quit Buggin' Me!

Name _____

April Fool's Day

Placing candy bugs in clever places is one fun way to trick your friends. Color each matching half of a bug the same color. You will need **six** different colors.

Changing Places

Name _____

April Fool's Day

Are you easily fooled?

Look **carefully** at the numbers. Write **ten** 3-digit number combinations inside the light bulbs using these numbers. One number may need to be flipped.

Page 40

Page 41

The Ol' Spider Joke

Name _____

April Fool's Day

"Oh, no! There's a giant, furry, ugly spider crawling up your back, and it's making a huge web!"

"Yeah, right!"

Discover the pattern in the spider web and fill in the missing numbers. No connecting numbers are ever the same.

Love Our Planet

Name _____

Earth Day

Use a **blue** crayon to color all of the spaces with **odd numbers**. Then begin at the ★. Write the letters that are **not** colored in the spaces below in the same clockwise order.

SAVE OUR EARTH
GET RID OF
POLLUTION!

Page 42

Page 43

IF8721 *Challenge Your Mind*

Save Our Water!

Name _____

Circle the word in each raindrop that comes **first** when counting. Then write its letter on the matching line below.

How do some children want to conserve water?

T H E Y   W A N T   T O
13th 9th 12th 1st   3rd 11th 14th 13th   13th 2nd

S T O P   T A K I N G
6th 13th 2nd 7th   13th 11th 10th 5th 14th 4th

B A T H S !
8th 11th 13th 9th 6th

Happy Birthday

Name _____

Solve the problems. Then add the five sums in the tree rings to find the age of each tree. Write this number on the line.

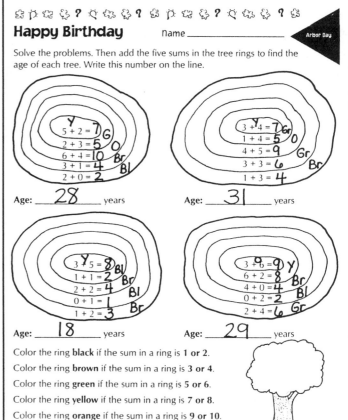

Tree 1 (Y, G, O, Br, Bl):
5 + 2 = 7
2 + 3 = 5
6 + 4 = 10
3 + 1 = 4
2 + 0 = 2

Age: **28** years

Tree 2 (Y, Gr, O, Gr, Br):
3 + 4 = 7
1 + 4 = 5
4 + 5 = 9
3 + 3 = 6
1 + 3 = 4

Age: **31** years

Tree 3 (Bl, Br, Bl, Br):
3 + 5 = 8
1 + 1 = 2
2 + 2 = 4
0 + 1 = 1
1 + 2 = 3

Age: **18** years

Tree 4 (Y, Br, Bl, Gr):
3 + 6 = 9
6 + 2 = 8
4 + 0 = 4
0 + 2 = 2
2 + 4 = 6

Age: **29** years

Color the ring **black** if the sum in a ring is **1 or 2**.
Color the ring **brown** if the sum in a ring is **3 or 4**.
Color the ring **green** if the sum in a ring is **5 or 6**.
Color the ring **yellow** if the sum in a ring is **7 or 8**.
Color the ring **orange** if the sum in a ring is **9 or 10**.

Tree-mendous Riddles

Name _____

Use a calculator to answer the riddles. Remember to press the equal sign after each direction and flip the calculator at the end to read the answer.

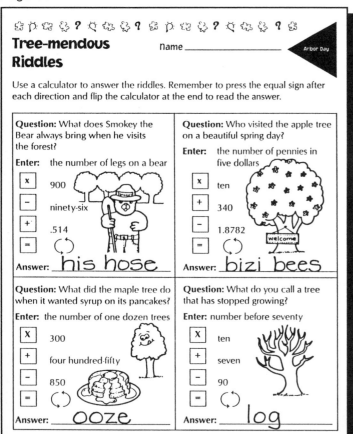

Question: What does Smokey the Bear always bring when he visits the forest?

Enter: the number of legs on a bear

x   900
−   ninety-six
+   .514
=

Answer: **his hose**

Question: Who visited the apple tree on a beautiful spring day?

Enter: the number of pennies in five dollars

x   ten
+   340
−   1.8782
=

Answer: **bizi bees**

Question: What did the maple tree do when it wanted syrup on its pancakes?

Enter: the number of one dozen trees

X   300
+   four hundred-fifty
−   850
=

Answer: **ooze**

Question: What do you call a tree that has stopped growing?

Enter: number before seventy

X   ten
+   seven
−   90
=

Answer: **log**

Home Sweet Home

Name _____

Follow the path and solve the problems to discover the number of trees in this forest.

Start   7   x   7   +   7

6   x   8   +

8   +   5   +   5

Answer **100**   =   10   +   6

Mother's Day Bouquet

Name _____

Mother's Day

Write each missing number.

Color the space **yellow** if the number is **1–5**.

Color the space **purple** if the number is **6–10**.

Color the space **orange** if the number is **11–15**.

Color the space **red** if the number is **16–20**.

Color the space **green** if the number is **21–25**.

Page 48

Mother Dear

Name _____

Mother's Day

Use a calculator to answer the questions. Remember to press the equal sign after each direction and flip the calculator at the end to read the answer.

Question: Who is one of the most famous mothers in history?

Enter: number of tentacles on an octopus

+	8,000
−	398
÷	twenty
×	92
=	↻

Answer: _Goose_

Question: What mother doesn't lecture her child for "piggy" table manners?

Enter: number of pennies in 3 quarters

×	ten
+	four
−	150
=	↻

Answer: _hog_

Question: What did her children say as she read her favorite nursery rhymes?

Enter: the number of inches in one foot

×	thirty
+	24
+	7,680
+	.01006
=	↻

Answer: _goo goo_

Question: What did this famous mother call her first child?

Enter: number of years in a century

×	six
+	two
−	134.0955
×	four
=	↻

Answer: _big egg_

Page 49

Honor Veterans

Name _____

Memorial Day

Solve these addition problems. Then match the letters on each star to the answers on the lines below.

I $2 + 6 + 3 =$ **11**

M $7 + 2 + 4 =$ **13**

C $4 + 6 + 6 =$ **16**

P $2 + 1 + 2 =$ **5**

Y $5 + 6 + 1 =$ **12**

S $5 + 4 + 6 =$ **15**

A $2 + 3 + 1 =$ **6**

R $9 + 6 + 4 =$ **19**

O $2 + 3 + 4 =$ **9**

N $1 + 0 + 2 =$ **3**

B $3 + 1 + 0 =$ **4**

D $8 + 6 + 4 =$ **18**

H $3 + 3 + 4 =$ **10**

T $1 + 0 + 1 =$ **2**

V $7 + 6 + 4 =$ **17**

L $5 + 6 + 3 =$ **14**

E $2 + 1 + 4 =$ **7**

W $3 + 3 + 2 =$ **8**

Why do Americans celebrate Memorial Day?

T O
‾2‾ ‾9‾

C E L E B R A T E
16 7 14 7 4 19 6 2 7

P E A C E   A N D
5 7 6 16 7   6 3 18

H O N O R   T H O S E
10 9 3 9 19   2 10 9 15 7

W H O   D I E D   I N
8 10 9   18 11 7 18   11 3

W A R S .
8 6 19 15

Page 50

Boom!

Name _____

Flag Day

Think big! Solve each subtraction problem. Then check them with a calculator.

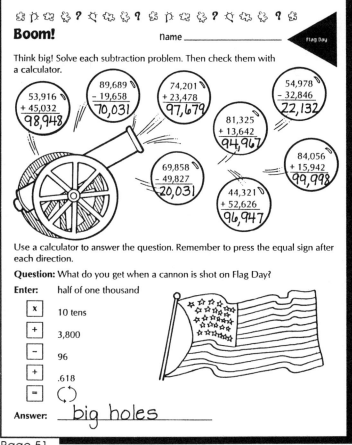

53,916
+ 45,032
98,948

89,689
− 19,658
70,031

74,201
+ 23,478
97,679

54,978
− 32,846
22,132

81,325
+ 13,642
94,967

69,858
− 49,827
20,031

84,056
+ 15,942
99,998

44,321
+ 52,626
96,947

Use a calculator to answer the question. Remember to press the equal sign after each direction.

Question: What do you get when a cannon is shot on Flag Day?

Enter: half of one thousand

×	10 tens
+	3,800
−	96
+	.618
=	↻

Answer: _big holes_

Page 51

© Instructional Fair • TS Denison

IF8721 *Challenge Your Mind*

We Salute You!

Name _____

Flag Day

Solve the addition and subtraction problems.

U 85 +15 = 100	
G 47 +83 = 130	O 52 −29 = 23
E 75 −37 = 38	n 38 +52 = 90
A 26 +28 = 54	J 63 −29 = 34
I 80 −16 = 64	W 25 +58 = 83
H 27 +58 = 85	V 72 −15 = 57
S 46 +27 = 73	T 91 −15 = 76
	E 19 +19 = 38
	A 72 −18 = 54

Match the letters in each box with the answers below each line to answer this question.

Proud Americans salute the U.S. flag. What does the flag do in return?

N O T H I N G . I T
90 23 76 85 64 90 130   64 76

J U S T W A V E S .
34 100 73 76   83 54 57 38 73

Page 52

Dad's "Outta This World!"

Name _____

Father's Day

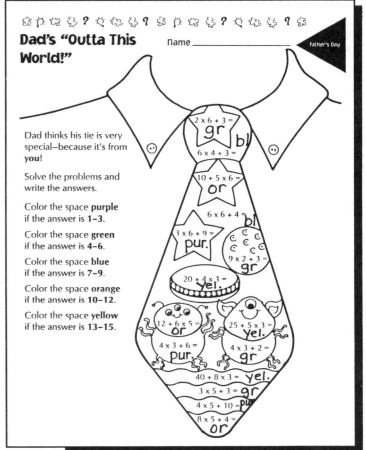

Dad thinks his tie is very special—because it's from **you!**

Solve the problems and write the answers.

Color the space **purple** if the answer is **1–3**.

Color the space **green** if the answer is **4–6**.

Color the space **blue** if the answer is **7–9**.

Color the space **orange** if the answer is **10–12**.

Color the space **yellow** if the answer is **13–15**.

Tie problems:
2 × 6 + 3 = gr   bl
6 × 4 + 3 =
10 + 5 × 6 = or
6 × 6 + 4 = bl
3 × 6 + 9 = pur.
9 × 2 + 3 = gr
20 + 4 × 3 = yel.
12 + 6 × 5 = or   25 + 5 × 3 = yel.
4 × 3 + 6 = pur.   4 × 3 + 2 = gr
40 + 8 × 3 = yel.
3 × 5 + 3 = gr
4 × 5 + 10 = pu
8 × 5 + 4 = or

Page 53

Dear Ol' Dad

Name _____

Father's Day

Use a calculator to answer the questions. Remember to press the equal key after each direction and flip the calculator at the end to read the answer.

Question: What's the main difference between a father and his young children?

Enter: half of one hundred
+ 16,000
÷ five
+ 5.514
=

Answer: his size

Question: What are Dad's favorite fish to catch?

Enter: eight thousand
+ 861
X six hundred
+ eighteen
=

Answer: biggies

Question: What are Dad's favorite words to his child on a fishing trip?

Enter: number of cents in one dollar
+ 180
÷ .05
− 1,200
+ forty-five
=

Answer: shhh

Question: What is a father's least favorite word from his child on a fishing trip in a boat?

Enter: number of cents in two quarters
+ 7,000
− 337
x eight
=

Answer: holes

Page 54

Superstar

Name _____

4th of July

Connect the dots. Start at **100** and **count by 10s**.

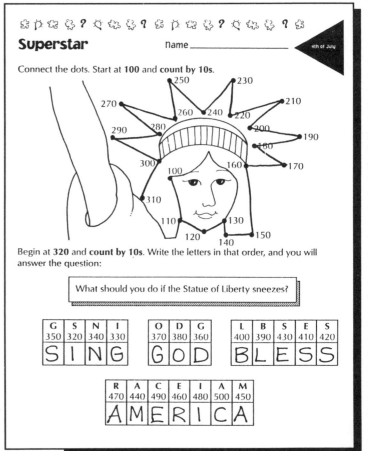

Begin at **320** and **count by 10s**. Write the letters in that order, and you will answer the question:

What should you do if the Statue of Liberty sneezes?

G	S	N	I
350	320	340	330
S	I	N	G

O	D	G
370	380	360
G	O	D

L	B	S	E	S
400	390	430	410	420
B	L	E	S	S

R	A	C	E	I	A	M
470	440	490	460	480	500	450
A	M	E	R	I	C	A

Page 55

IF8721 *Challenge Your Mind*

Rockets Red Glare

Name _____

Solve the multiplication problems. Match the letters to the answers on the lines below.

What did one firecracker say to the other firecracker?

A 7
× 7
49

B 3
× 2
6

E 6
× 4
24

H 5
× 8
40

I 3
× 7
21

G 9
× 8
72

T 9
× 9
81

P 3
× 4
12

M 5
× 3
15

n 4
× 4
16

u 4
× 7
28

R 10
× 5
50

y 5
× 6
30

S 7
× 6
42

O 8
× 7
56

M Y   P O P   I S
15 30   12 30 12   21 42

B I G G E R   T H A N
6 21 72 72 24 50   81 40 49 16

Y O U R S !
30 56 28 50 42

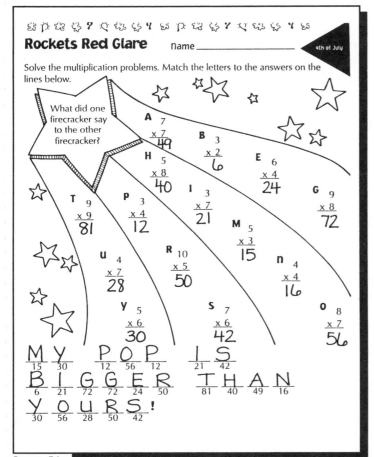

Page 56

Independence Day Parade

Name _____

Get into the spirit of the 4th of July and decorate your bike!

Color the space **red** if the number is **even**.

Color the space **blue** if the number is **odd**.

Color or leave the space **white** if the space contains no number.

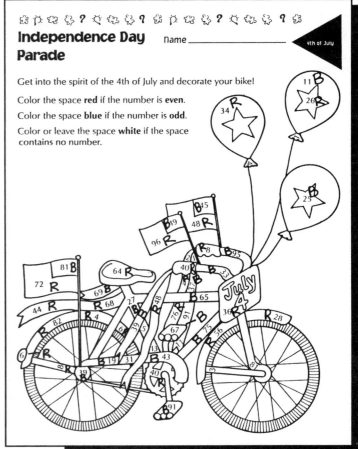

Page 57

Say "Uncle!"

Name _____

Solve the problems.

Color the space **red** if the answer is **greater than 50**.

Color the space **blue** if the answer is **between 1 and 49**.

Color or leave the space **white** if the answer is **50**.

Color the space **tan** if the answer is **0**.

Page 58

What a Dandy!

Name _____

Solve the word problems. Answer the riddle by matching the letters to the answers. Then connect the dots in order from smallest to largest.

How can you make a Yankee Doodle?

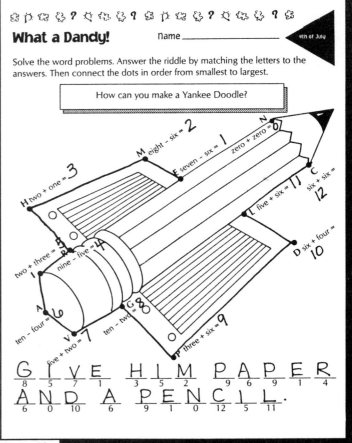

G I V E   H I M   P A P E R
8 5 7 1   3 5 2   6 9 1 4

A N D   A   P E N C I L .
6 0 10   6   9 1 0 12 5 11

Page 59

My Cup of Tea

Name _____

4th of July

Begin at **3** and count by **3s**. Write the letters in that order on the teacups, and you will answer the question:

> What was the American colonists' favorite tea?

E	Y	T	H
9	12	3	6

THEY

D	L	E	I	K
27	15	24	18	21

LIKED

T	R	I	H	E
30	42	39	33	36

THEIR

I	Y	B	L	T	E	R
48	63	51	45	60	54	57

LIBERTY

Count by **3s** and connect the dots.

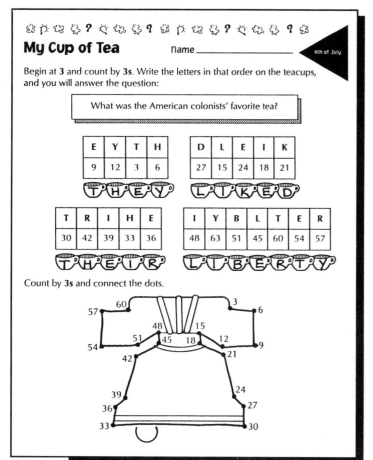

Page 60

So Proudly We Hail

Name _____

4th of July

Solve the multiplication problems. Match the letters to the answers on the lines below to solve the riddle.

> Why did Paul Revere ride his horse through town shouting, "The British are coming"?

THE HORSE WAS
142 156 99 156 128 164 219 99

MUCH TOO HEAVY
85 168 25 156 128 128 156 99 48 546 328

TO CARRY.
142 128 25 48 164 164 328

Page 61

A Loud Cry

Name _____

4th of July

Solve the division problems. Then match the letters and answers to the numbers on the lines below, and you will figure out the riddle.

> Why did Paul Revere bring a handkerchief to Boston?

TO GIVE TO THE
4 1 2 6 10 3 4 8 7

TOWN CRIER
4 1 9 3 11 5 3 7

Page 62

Just a Minute, Man!

Name _____

4th of July

Write the time shown on each clock. Try to do this in one minute or less while someone times you.

9:45   6:30   7:15   4:35   8:50

7:25   3:00   11:10   12:40   2:20

8:05   1:55   4:30   5:35   9:15

How do you rate as a Minuteman?	
Number Correct	**Rank**
15	Split Secondman
13–14	Merry Minuteman
11–12	Sluggish, but Hard-Working Hourman
10 or less	Dozing Dayman

Page 63

© Instructional Fair • TS Denison

IF8721 *Challenge Your Mind*

Don't Give Up!

Name _____

Labor Day

Circle the **smallest** number in each bottle. Use the code at the bottom of the page to write the letter on each line.

What job is very easy to stick to?

Bottles row 1: 753/**735** → W | **821**/830 → O | 141/**137** → R | **381**/390 → K | **232**/321 → I | 991/**919** → N | 856/**685** → G

Bottles row 2: 322/**232** → I | **919**/920 → N | **106**/160 → A | **685**/692 → G | 871/**786** → L | 463/**436** → U | 216/**260** → E

Bottles row 3: 521/**529**... **521**/529 → F | 165/**106** → A | 494/**501** → C | 981/**987** → T | 850/**821** → O | 153/**137** → R | 625/**619** → Y

Code

106	494	216	521	685	232	381	786	919	821	137	981	436	735	619
A	C	E	F	G	I	K	L	N	O	R	T	U	W	Y

Page 64

Taking It Easy

Name _____

Labor Day

Solve the number problems. Match the letters and the answers to the numbers on the lines below.

Why is working in a rubber band factory one of the easiest jobs in the world?

A	B	C	E
$56 + 9 = 65$	$78 - 59 = 19$	$67 - 29 = 38$	$28 + 67 = 95$

H	I	n	P
$45 - 18 = 27$	$72 + 18 = 90$	$83 - 15 = 68$	$54 + 16 = 70$

S	T	u	A
$66 + 14 = 80$	$33 - 15 = 18$	$59 + 19 = 78$	$90 - 25 = 65$

B E C A U S E   I T ' S
19 95 38 65 78 80 95   90 18 80

S U C H   A   S N A P !
80 78 38 27   65   80 68 65 70

Page 65

Fishing and Sailing

Name _____

Labor Day

Solve each problem. Write the answer in the box.

Color the fish **red** if the answer is **1–5**.

Color the fish **yellow** if the answer is **6–10**.

Color the fish **blue** if the answer is **11–15**.

Color the fish **purple** if the answer is **16–20**.

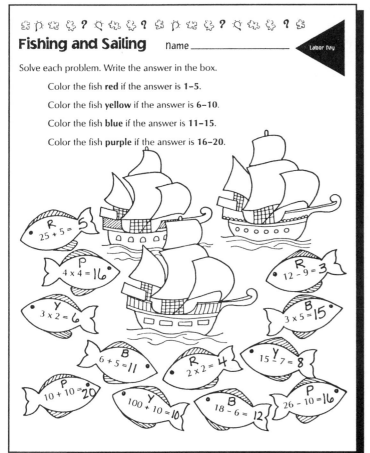

R: $25 \div 5 = 5$
P: $4 \times 4 = 16$
R: $12 - 9 = 3$
Y: $3 \times 2 = 6$
B: $3 \times 5 = 15$
B: $6 + 5 = 11$
R: $2 \times 2 = 4$
Y: $15 - 7 = 8$
P: $10 + 10 = 20$
Y: $100 \div 10 = 10$
B: $18 - 6 = 12$
P: $26 - 10 = 16$

Page 66

Flags of the United Nations

Name _____

United Nations Day

Color the space **orange** if the number is **1–25**.

Color the space **red** if the number is **26–50**.

Color the space **black** if the number is **51–75**.

Color the space **yellow** if the number is **76–100**.

Color the space **green** if the number is **101–125**.

Color the space **blue** if the number is **126–150**.

Color or leave the space **white** if the number is **151–175**.

B = blue

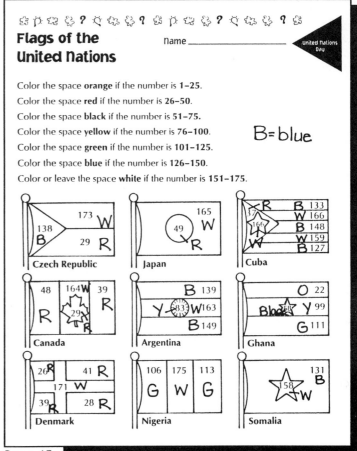

Czech Republic: 173 W, 138 B, 29 R

Japan: 165 W, 49 × R

Cuba: R, B 133, W 166, 166, B 148, W 159, W, B 127

Canada: 48, 164 W, 39, 29, R, R

Argentina: B 139, Y-83-W 163, B 149

Ghana: O 22, Black, Y 99, G 111

Denmark: 26, 41 R, 171 W, 39 R, 28 R

Nigeria: 106 | 175 | 113, G W G

Somalia: 131 B, 158, W

Page 67

© Instructional Fair • TS Denison

IF8721 *Challenge Your Mind*

Olive Branch of Peace

Name _____

Solve each problem. Write the answers in the boxes. Then match the letters and the answers to the numbers on the lines below.

M 6 + 6 + 2 + 3 **9**

I 5 + 8 − 3 × 2 **20**

T 18 − 9 × 3 + 1 **28**

U 10 × 4 + 5 + 6 **14**

D 6 × 6 − 6 + 5 **6**

O 12 ÷ 4 × 3 + 9 **18**

P 14 − 5 × 2 + 3 **21**

A 25 + 5 × 2 + 1 **11**

L 3 × 3 + 9 − 3 **15**

What animal can sometimes be seen in the United Nations building?

A D I P L O - M U T T
11 6 20 21 15 18 9 14 28 28

Page 68

I Need My Mummy!

name _____

Each mummy is wrapped in **five** bandages marked A, B, C, D, and E. Write the two numbers on each bandage. Add them to find the length of each bandage.

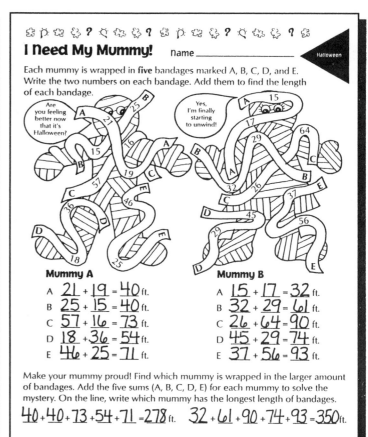

Mummy A

A 21 + 19 = 40 ft.
B 25 + 15 = 40 ft.
C 57 + 16 = 73 ft.
D 18 + 36 = 54 ft.
E 46 + 25 = 71 ft.

Mummy B

A 15 + 17 = 32 ft.
B 32 + 29 = 61 ft.
C 26 + 64 = 90 ft.
D 45 + 29 = 74 ft.
E 37 + 56 = 93 ft.

Make your mummy proud! Find which mummy is wrapped in the larger amount of bandages. Add the five sums (A, B, C, D, E) for each mummy to solve the mystery. On the line, write which mummy has the longest length of bandages.

40 + 40 + 73 + 54 + 71 = 278 ft.   32 + 61 + 90 + 74 + 93 = 350 ft.

Page 69

A Boo-tiful Parade

Name _____

Follow the directions. Begin with the first ghost in the bottom left corner.

Directions:

1. Color a **red number 1** on the **first** ghost.

2. Draw **silly orange hats** on the **fifth** and **seventh** ghosts.

3. Color **purple polka-dots** on the **ninth** ghost.

4. Color **green stripes** on the **third** ghost.

5. Write **"Boo"** on the **tenth** ghost.

6. Draw a **big tooth** in the **second** ghost's mouth.

7. Draw **funny yellow hair** on the **fourth** ghost's head.

8. Draw **black beards** on the **sixth** and **eighth** ghosts.

Page 70

Count on Me!

name _____

Help Igor and Agar get ready for Halloween by coloring some of their fingernails. Always begin on the left side.

IGOR

1. Count by 2s on Igor's fingers.
2. Outline those fingernails in **orange**.
3. How many are orange? **12**
4. There are **12** two's in 24.
5. Write the outlined letters on the lines below.

AGAR

1. Count by 3s on Agar's fingers.
2. Outline those fingernails in **black**.
3. How many are black? **8**
4. There are **8** three's in 24.
5. Write the outlined letters on the lines below.

How does a monster count?

O N I T S
F I N G E R S
- O F C O U R S E !

Why don't they use their feet?
(Write the remaining letters on their fingers.)

S M E L L T H E I R
T O E S A N D Y O U
W I L L K N O W !

Page 71

Get the Point?

Name _____

Halloween

Color each character's hair and matching hat the same. You will need ten different colors.

Monster Treats

Name _____

Halloween

Frank and Stein are sorting their Halloween treats. They have already separated them into groups of the same kind. If the treats are shared equally, how many pieces of each kind will each monster get?

Circle every two treats. Write the division problem and solve it. The first one is done for you.

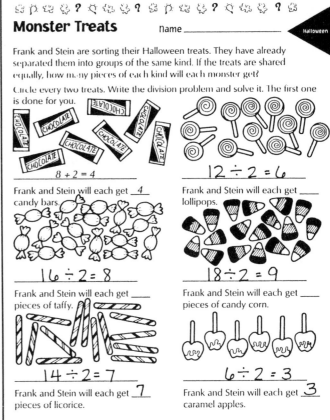

$8 \div 2 = 4$

Frank and Stein will each get __4__ candy bars.

$12 \div 2 = 6$

Frank and Stein will each get ____ lollipops.

$16 \div 2 = 8$

Frank and Stein will each get ____ pieces of taffy.

$18 \div 2 = 9$

Frank and Stein will each get ____ pieces of candy corn.

$14 \div 2 = 7$

Frank and Stein will each get __7__ pieces of licorice.

$6 \div 2 = 3$

Frank and Stein will each get __3__ caramel apples.

Color Me Boo-tiful!

Name _____

Halloween

Solve the addition problems and color each bone as directed.

34–orange   97–red   56–green
75–black   48–yellow   83–purple

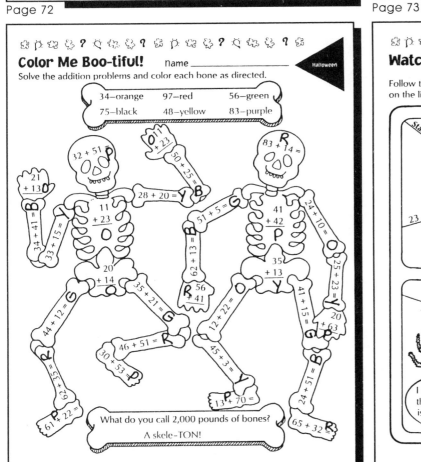

What do you call 2,000 pounds of bones?
A skele-TON!

Watch Your Step!

Name _____

Halloween

Follow the directions to trace the path of each spider on its web. Stay on the lines of the web.

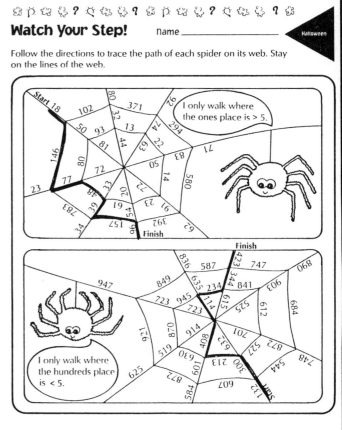

I only walk where the ones place is > 5.

I only walk where the hundreds place is < 5.

Give Me "Five!"

Halloween

Hope you have a pencil "handy." Begin at **55** and count by **5s** to connect the dots.

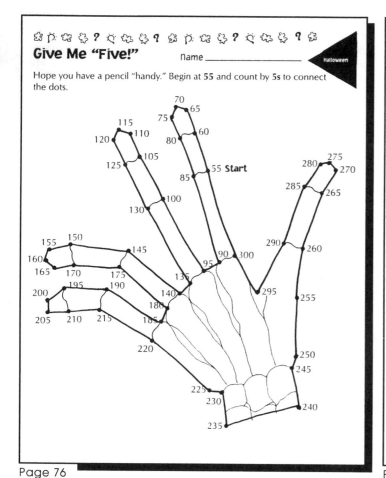

Midnight Snack

Name _____

Halloween

Solve the subtraction problems. Write the letters on the lines.

What do you call a mummy who eats crackers in bed?

A C R U M M Y   M U M M Y
26 12 42 73 11 33 15   11 43 54 64 23

M	M	A	C
97 – 43 54	68 – 35 33	48 – 22 26	36 – 24 12
Y	**M**	**M**	**R**
79 – 64 15	97 – 33 64	75 – 64 11	56 – 14 42
Y	**U**	**M**	**U**
54 – 31 23	83 – 10 73	45 – 34 11	66 – 23 43

Glowing Grins

Name _____

Halloween

Add the three numbers in each jack-o'-lantern's eyes and nose.
Write the answer in its mouth.

Color the jack-o'-lantern **orange** if the number is **even**.

Color the jack-o'-lantern **black** if the number is **odd**.

Sailing... Sailing...

Name _____

Columbus Day

Circle the **smallest** number in each sail.

Box the **largest** number in each sail.

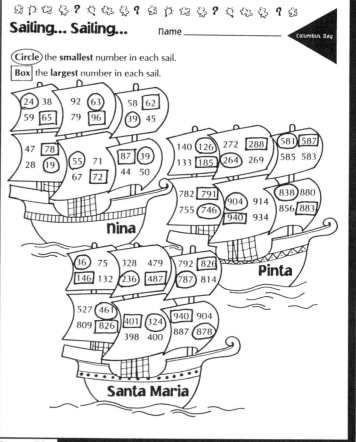

Birds of a Feather

Name _____

Thanksgiving

Write the missing signs (+, –, =) in each feather. Use the answers and color key to color them.

3 = yellow	7 = orange	
4 = blue	8 = green	
5 = red	9 = purple	

Ticklish Situation

Name _____

Thanksgiving

How many feathers does each turkey have? Read the clues and write the numbers on the lines.

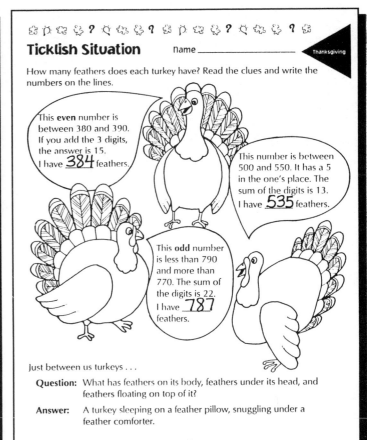

This **even** number is between 380 and 390. If you add the 3 digits, the answer is 15. I have __384__ feathers.

This number is between 500 and 550. It has a 5 in the one's place. The sum of the digits is 13. I have __535__ feathers.

This **odd** number is less than 790 and more than 770. The sum of the digits is 22. I have __787__ feathers.

Just between us turkeys . . .

Question: What has feathers on its body, feathers under its head, and feathers floating on top of it?

Answer: A turkey sleeping on a feather pillow, snuggling under a feather comforter.

All Wrapped Up

Name _____

Thanksgiving

Solve the problems by providing the missing number.

Across

2. $2 \times \boxed{6} = 12$

4. $39 - 31 = \boxed{8}$

7. $14 + \boxed{7} = 21$

8. $16 + 4 = \boxed{4}$

9. $100 \times \boxed{1} = 100$

Down

1. 256 = 2 hundreds + $\boxed{5}$ tens + 6 ones

3. $\boxed{10} + 73 = 83$

5. $18 + \boxed{2} = 9$

6. 83 = 8 tens + $\boxed{3}$ ones

10. $\boxed{9} \times 9 = 81$

Write the number words 1–10 in this puzzle.

(crossword)
```
      F
   S  I  X       E I G H T       T
      V           W        H
   S  E  V  E  N           R
              F O U R      E E
              O  N  E      E
                           N
                           I
                           N
                           E
```

Use this code for a special message.

one	two	three	four	five	six	seven	eight	nine	ten
O	A	E	G	F	L	D	I	N	S

What did the leftover turkey drumstick say?

F O I L E D   A G A I N !
five one eight six three seven   two four two eight nine

...And the Winner Is...

Name _____

Thanksgiving

Solve the problems. Then place an X on the turkey in each pair that weighs more.

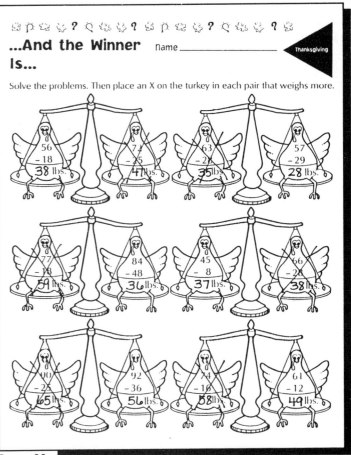

56 – 18 = 38 lbs.	74 – 25 = 49 lbs.
63 – 28 = 35 lbs.	57 – 29 = 28 lbs.
77 – 18 = 59 lbs.	84 – 48 = 36 lbs.
45 – 8 = 37 lbs.	66 – 28 = 38 lbs.
90 – 25 = 65 lbs.	92 – 36 = 56 lbs.
74 – 16 = 58 lbs.	61 – 12 = 49 lbs.

© Instructional Fair • TS Denison

IF8721 Challenge Your Mind

Let's Get Corny!

Name _____

Thanksgiving

Use a **yellow** crayon to circle hidden division facts (→, ↑, ↓). Write them on the lines below. One is done for you.

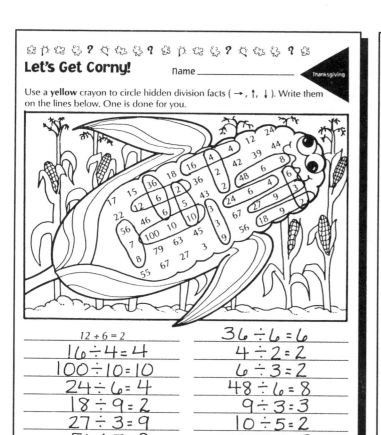

$12 \div 6 = 2$	$36 \div 6 = 6$
$16 \div 4 = 4$	$4 \div 2 = 2$
$100 \div 10 = 10$	$6 \div 3 = 2$
$24 \div 6 = 4$	$48 \div 6 = 8$
$18 \div 9 = 2$	$9 \div 3 = 3$
$27 \div 3 = 9$	$10 \div 5 = 2$
$56 \div 7 = 8$	$27 \div 9 = 3$

Page 84

Please, Pass the Pumpkin Pie

Name _____

Thanksgiving

Help Grandma make **six** whole pumpkin pies by connecting the pieces that go together. Then write the letter from each piece on the line above the matching fraction below.

Why didn't the turkey want a piece of pumpkin pie?

H	E	W	A	S		S	T	U	F	F	E	D
$\frac{1}{6}$	$\frac{1}{5}$	$\frac{1}{4}$	$\frac{2}{7}$	$\frac{1}{3}$		$\frac{5}{12}$	$\frac{7}{12}$	$\frac{2}{3}$	$\frac{5}{7}$	$\frac{3}{4}$	$\frac{4}{5}$	$\frac{5}{6}$

Page 85

Food for Thought

Name _____

Thanksgiving

Solve the addition and subtraction problems. Use the code to write the letters that match the missing numbers.

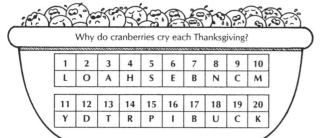

Why do cranberries cry each Thanksgiving?

1	2	3	4	5	6	7	8	9	10
L	O	A	H	S	E	B	N	C	M

11	12	13	14	15	16	17	18	19	20
Y	D	T	R	P	I	B	U	C	K

$+\frac{\boxed{3}}{7}$ $-\frac{\boxed{6}}{5}$ $-\frac{18}{9}$ $-\frac{\boxed{3}}{3}$ $-\frac{\boxed{18}}{9}$ $+\frac{4}{\boxed{5}}$ $-\frac{11}{5}$
$\overline{10}$ $\overline{}$ $\overline{9}$ $\overline{}$ $\overline{}$ $\overline{}$ $\overline{6}$
B   E   C   A   U   S   E

$-\frac{\boxed{20}}{10}$ $-\frac{\boxed{16}}{7}$ $-\frac{\boxed{12}}{8}$ $-\frac{13}{8}$ $+\frac{9}{6}$ $-\frac{\boxed{16}}{9}$ $-\frac{14}{\boxed{9}}$ $-\frac{\boxed{20}}{10}$
$\overline{}$ $\overline{}$ $\overline{5}$ $\overline{15}$ $\overline{5}$ $\overline{}$
K   I   D   S   P   I   C   K

$-\frac{\boxed{2}}{2}$ $-\frac{15}{\boxed{8}}$ $-\frac{\boxed{13}}{8}$ $-\frac{13}{\boxed{4}}$ $+\frac{\boxed{6}}{9}$ $-\frac{13}{15}$
$\overline{0}$ $\overline{7}$ $\overline{5}$ $\overline{9}$ $\overline{15}$ $\overline{10}$!
O   N   T   H   E   M

Page 86

Anyone Home?

Name _____

Thanksgiving

Cut out each triangle. Place each side of a triangle next to the side of another triangle with the answer. (**Note:** The sides that have no numbers are outside edges.) To begin, place the triangle with the sun at the top. See if you can create a tepee.

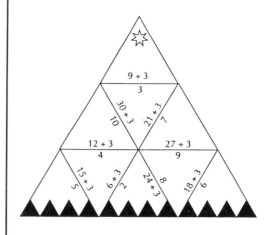

Page 87

© Instructional Fair • TS Denison

IF8721 *Challenge Your Mind*

M–M–M–MMM!

name _____

Thanksgiving

Help the Indians and Pilgrims calculate how much food to prepare for their feast. Write each answer on the line below the problem.

$78 + 22 + 10 + 15$
25 turkeys

$5 \times 9 + 27 - 12$ = **60** ears of corn-on-the-cob

$15 + 10 + 5$
5 deer

$75 + 55 \times 2 - 100$
160 carrots

$25 \times 4 + 100 + 2$
100 potatoes

$99 - 53 + 2$
23 loaves of bread

$100 \times 10 + 2 - 150$
350 beans

$20 \times 5 + 2 + 6$
56 apples

Page 88

Stepping in the Right Direction

name _____

Thanksgiving

Look at the footsteps headed toward the Thanksgiving feast. Add <, or >, or = between each footprint. One is done for you.

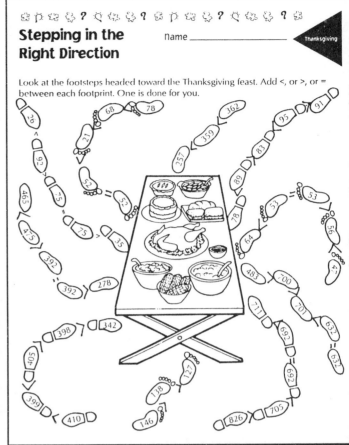

Page 89

Lighting the Mishumaa Saba

name _____

Kwanzaa

Solve the equations. Write each answer in the box.

Color the space **black** if the missing number is **0–2**.
Color the space **red** if the missing number is **3–5**.
Color the space **green** if the missing number is **6–8**.
Color the space **yellow** if the missing number is **9–11**.
Color the space **orange** if the missing number is **12–15**.

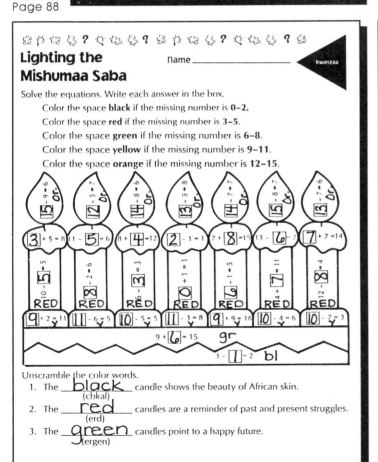

Unscramble the color words.
1. The ___**black**___ candle shows the beauty of African skin.
   (cbkal)
2. The ___**red**___ candles are a reminder of past and present struggles.
   (erd)
3. The ___**green**___ candles point to a happy future.
   (ergen)

Page 90

Vibunzi

name _____

Kwanzaa

Vibunzi are dried ears of corn. They represent the children in a family, who are the hope of the future.

Write the missing signs (<, >, =).
Color the kernel **red** if the sign is <.
Color the kernel **black** if the sign is >.
Color the kernel **yellow** if the sign is =.

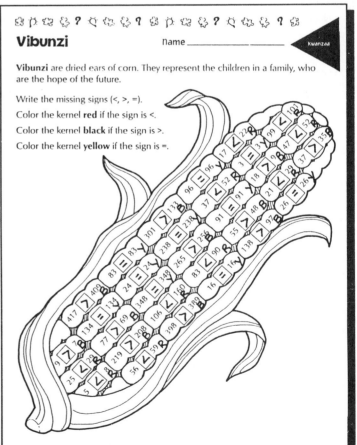

Page 91

© Instructional Fair • TS Denison

IF8721 *Challenge Your Mind*

Swahili Speech

name _____

Solve each multiplication problem. Write each answer on the line. Use the code to spell Swahili words that are used during the Kwanzaa holiday. Write the letter in each box that matches the number in the code below.

9	9	4	4	6
x 3	x 4	x 4	x 9	x 6
27	36	16	36	36
J	A	M	A	A

(family)

6	9	3	2	3	4
x 5	x 9	x 5	x 9	x 3	x 8
30	81	15	18	9	32
U	P	E	N	D	O

(love)

4	5	2	10	3	8	12
x 5	x 3	x 4	x 2	x 8	x 2	x 3
20	15	8	20	24	16	36
H	E	S	H	I	M	A

(pride)

6	9	7	6
x 8	x 4	x 7	x 4
48	36	49	24
K	A	Z	I

(work)

3	3	8	6	2	4
x 4	x10	x 5	x 6	x10	x 9
12	30	40	36	20	36
F	U	R	A	H	A

(happiness)

3	2	6	9	4
x12	x 8	x 6	x 2	x 6
36	16	36	18	24
A	M	A	N	I

(peace)

2	8	8	5	12	10	6
x 4	x 3	x 6	x 6	x 4	x 3	x 5
8	24	48	30	48	30	30
S	I	K	U	K	U	U

(holiday)

4	12	2	2	9
x 4	x 2	x 5	x 5	x 4
16	24	10	10	36
M	I	L	A

(tradition)

Code

A	D	E	F	H	I	J	K	L	M	N	O	P	R	S	U	Z
36	9	15	12	20	24	27	48	10	16	18	32	81	40	8	30	49

Twelve Days of Christmas

name _____

Complete each number sentence so that the two numbers in each picture equal the number in the song. Use +, −, x, or ÷. The first number sentence is done for you.

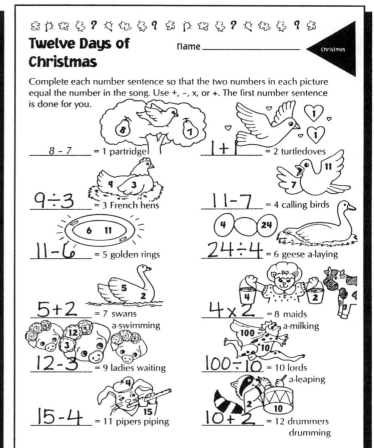

8 − 7 = 1 partridge

1 + 1 = 2 turtledoves

9 ÷ 3 = 3 French hens

11 − 7 = 4 calling birds

11 − 6 = 5 golden rings

24 ÷ 4 = 6 geese a-laying

5 + 2 = 7 swans a-swimming

4 x 2 = 8 maids a-milking

12 − 3 = 9 ladies waiting

100 ÷ 10 = 10 lords a-leaping

15 − 4 = 11 pipers piping

10 + 2 = 12 drummers drumming

Frosty the Snowman

name _____

Frosty the Snowman and his friends need a few items. Start at the top left and follow the directions carefully, but don't take too long or the page may melt!

1. Draw 3 coal buttons on the 1st, 3rd, 4th, and 7th snowmen.

2. Put a baseball cap on the 2nd, 5th, and 8th snowmen.

3. Wrap a big scarf around the necks of the 4th, 6th, and 10th snowmen.

4. Color orange carrot noses on the snowmen that **follow** the 3rd, 7th, and 9th snowmen.

5. Draw a coal nose on the rest of the snowmen.

6. Place a black top hat on Frosty's head. (**Hint:** He has a scarf, 3 buttons, and a carrot nose.)

Season for Singing

name _____

Circle the **largest** number in each musical note. Use the code below to write the matching letter on the line in each note.

What song does a peanut butter sandwich sing each Christmas?

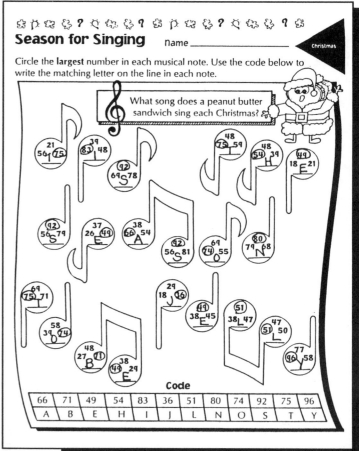

Code

66	71	49	54	83	36	51	80	74	92	75	96
A	B	E	H	I	J	L	N	O	S	T	Y

Use a calculator to answer the questions. Remember to press the equal key after each direction and flip the calculator at the end to read the answer.

Question: What does Santa say as he plants snow peas in his garden?

Enter: the number of pounds in 3 short tons

x	five hundred
+	40,000
+	four hundred
+	4
=	↻

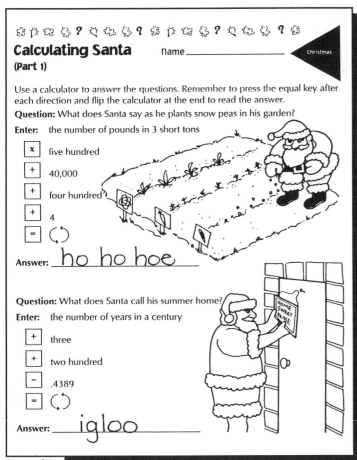

Answer: ho ho hoe

Question: What does Santa call his summer home?

Enter: the number of years in a century

+	three
+	two hundred
−	.4389
=	↻

Answer: igloo

Use a calculator to answer the questions. Remember to press the equal key after each direction.

Question: How does Santa's voice change when he's getting a sore throat?

Enter: one thousand

+	656
+	.1656
+	four thousand
=	↻

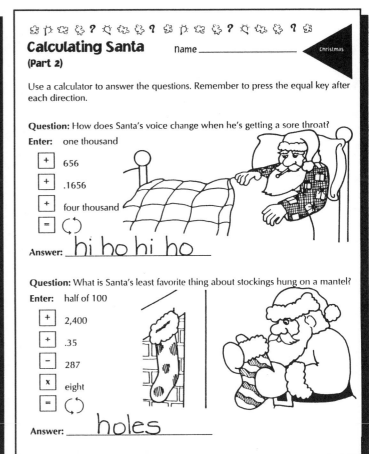

Answer: hi ho hi ho

Question: What is Santa's least favorite thing about stockings hung on a mantel?

Enter: half of 100

+	2,400
+	.35
−	287
x	eight
=	↻

Answer: holes

Solve the subtraction problems. Match the letters to the answers to solve the riddle.

A L B E R T
31 424 115 202 11 321

P I N E S T E I N
527 67 112 202 199 321 202 67 112

What is the name of the world's smartest Christmas tree?

A	B	E	I
156 −125 = 31	262 −147 = 115	325 −123 = 202	565 −498 = 67

L	n	P	R
878 −454 = 424	732 −620 = 112	655 −128 = 527	904 −893 = 11

S	T	E	n
395 −196 = 199	826 −505 = 321	468 −266 = 202	590 −478 = 112

Solve the addition problems. Write the letters on the lines.

T H E Y   H A V E
912 839 639 990   839 379 469 639

P R E S E N T
809 699 639 836 639 889 912

D R E A M S !
983 699 639 379 904 836

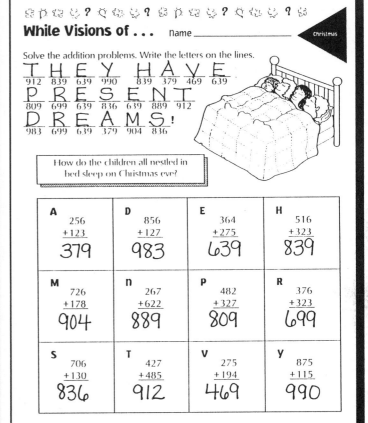

How do the children all nestled in bed sleep on Christmas eve?

A	D	E	H
256 +123 = 379	856 +127 = 983	364 +275 = 639	516 +323 = 839

M	n	P	R
726 +178 = 904	267 +622 = 889	482 +327 = 809	376 +323 = 699

S	T	V	Y
706 +130 = 836	427 +485 = 912	275 +194 = 469	875 +115 = 990

What Bugs Santa?   Name _____

Solve the multiplication problems. Then connect the answers in order from **largest** to **smallest**.

What insect really scares Santa?

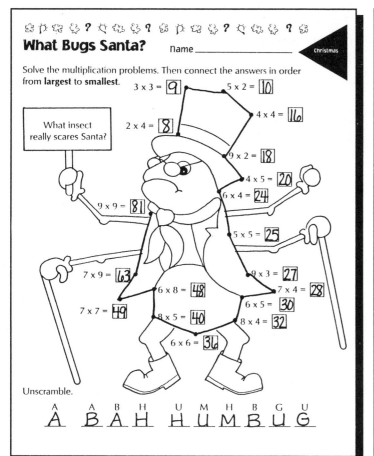

$3 \times 3 = \boxed{9}$
$5 \times 2 = \boxed{10}$
$2 \times 4 = \boxed{8}$
$4 \times 4 = \boxed{16}$
$9 \times 2 = \boxed{18}$
$4 \times 5 = \boxed{20}$
$6 \times 4 = \boxed{24}$
$9 \times 9 = \boxed{81}$
$5 \times 5 = \boxed{25}$
$9 \times 3 = \boxed{27}$
$7 \times 9 = \boxed{63}$
$7 \times 4 = \boxed{28}$
$6 \times 8 = \boxed{48}$
$6 \times 5 = \boxed{30}$
$7 \times 7 = \boxed{49}$
$8 \times 5 = \boxed{40}$
$8 \times 4 = \boxed{32}$
$6 \times 6 = \boxed{36}$

Unscramble.

A B B H U M H B G U
A BAH HUMBUG

Page 100

Trip up North   Name _____

Find the safest way to travel to the North Pole. Follow the clues to connect the dots. Be careful! Not all numbers will be used.

Clues

1. 6 tens = **60**
2. The number in the hundreds place in 849 **8**
3. 900 + 50 + 6 = 9 **5** 6
4. 7 hundreds = **700**
5. The number in the tens place in 934 **3**
6. 400 + 60 + 1 = 46 **1**
7. 2 ones = **2**
8. 2 hundreds + 9 tens + 5 ones = 200 + **90** + 5

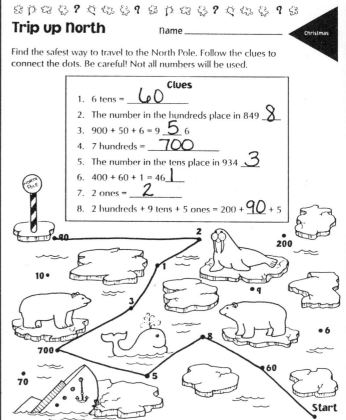

Page 101

A Special Glow   Name _____

Find the missing part of each candle to make it whole. Color it the same color as the part shown in the **menorah** (candle holder).

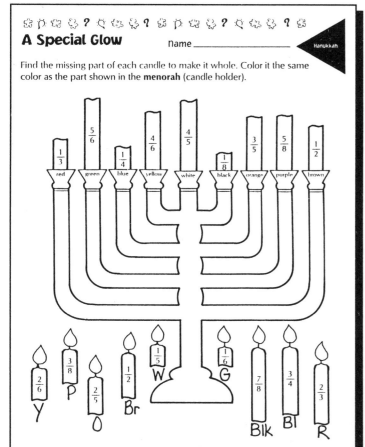

Page 102

Take a Spin   Name _____

"I'll spin the dreidel, and I'll see,
What stays in the pot and what's left for me!"

Read the definition of each dreidel symbol. Then study each game and fill in the missing blanks.

Dreidel Symbols

נ = Nun (none):   Player takes nothing.

ג = Gimmel (give):   Player takes everything in the pot. All players then add one more object to the pot.

ה = Heh (half):   Player takes half of the pot. If there's an odd number in the pot, the player takes the larger half.

ש = Shin (add):   Player adds one object to the pot.

Game 1

Four children are playing dreidel with pieces of candy. Thirty pieces remain in the pot. It is Isaac's turn. He spins ה and receives **15** piece(s) of candy. That leaves **15** piece(s) in the pot.

Next, Hannah spins ש. She must add **1** piece(s) to the pot. Now the pot has **16** piece(s) of candy.

Tommy takes his turn, and the dreidel shows ה. He gets **8** piece(s) of candy while **8** piece(s) remain in the pot.

Then Susie spins ג. She takes **8** piece(s) of candy. The number of pieces in the pot has changed to **0**, until each child adds one piece making the pot contain **4** piece(s).

Game 2

Mark, Kathy, and Bernie are using bottle caps in their dreidel game. At this point the pot has 23 bottle caps.

Mark frowns after he spins נ because he receives **0** bottle cap(s) while the pot has **23**. Then Kathy spins ה. Because she gets the larger half, she takes **12** bottle cap(s) and leaves **11** in the pot. Bernie spins ש. This changes the number of bottle caps in the pot to **12**.

Page 103
